Living in Light of the Victory

Due to difficulty obtaining copyright permission,
all Scripture has been taken from the King James
Version of the Bible.

Table of Contents

Acknowledgements

There are a great number of people I am indebted to who in one way or another aided in the production of this book. It would be impossible to list everyone, so I will name a few of the folks who helped bring this book to life.

Rod Fisher, your prayers and encouraging words were often used to spur me on to continue writing. Your encouragement is a large part of why I had the strength to finish what I had started.

River Church, you have been a great source of encouragement to me. I have grown tremendously because of all of you. Many of you have challenged me in very profound ways. I am continually challenged and encouraged by a great many of you. I am forever grateful for your love and support.

Jason Everhart and Kathie Rollins, thank you for encouraging me to use my gifts. Thank you for not allowing me to waste the gifts God has given to me. I have a habit of being slow to listen. Your habit of persistently, patiently and graciously speaking truth into my life is a huge blessing.

Jim Lowrey and Sharee Smith, thank you for reminding me to keep my writing simple.

Joey Yokeley, thank you for ripping out of my hands my excuses for not using the gifts God has given me. Thank you for the wisdom and encouragement you continually pour into my life. Thank you for giving me the freedom to use my gifts in our church body.

To my family, this book would not have been possible without all of you. I have been blessed with both sides of my family having a long legacy of faithfulness to Christ. I have seen you all live out this book. Your faithful witness, wisdom, love and encouragement have had a huge impact on my life. You all have shown me the practical impact that faith in Christ has on our daily life. You are all people who humbly and quietly serve and love the people God places in your path. I am continually amazed and blessed to be part of such an awesome legacy. It is quite humbling. Thank you. I love you guys!

Dedication

To Mom, Dad, Jennifer, Scott, Ashon and Braylon. The way you love people and live out your faith never ceases to amaze me. You are living testimonies of the goodness of God. I love you all very much!

Introduction

Readings: Philippians 2:12-3; 3:17-20

I will never forget my first experience visiting a foreign country. Upon arriving in Prague, before we even left the airport, I realized how drastically culture shapes the way we think and live. During those first few days I learned that a lot of things I assumed all people did or thought were, in fact, not what all people did or thought. It was shocking and disorienting to discover how radically different culture in the Czech Republic is from American culture. Living in the Czech Republic meant having to adopt a new way of life. There were new ways of doing things that I had to get used to. There were cultural assumptions that I was forced to let go of. My American ways simply would not mesh with a Czech way of life. I was put into a new culture, so I had to adapt to where I had been placed.

James' letter in the New Testament is like a guidebook on cultural etiquette. It is like a book written to help us adapt to the way of life in God's Kingdom. The Apostle Paul wrote to the church in Philippi telling them that they are citizens of heaven. When we become a Christian, we have a change in citizenship. Our citizenship moves from the Kingdom of this world to the Kingdom of God. We are still living in this world, but our citizenship has changed. We live in this world, but we are no longer ruled by this world. We belong to Christ. He is whom we are ruled by. King Jesus has taken us captive. We still live in this world, but we are part of a spiritual Kingdom. James wrote his letter to teach us how to live as citizens of this new, heavenly culture. He wrote his letter to draw a sharp contrast between the culture of our old Kingdom and the culture of the new Kingdom of which we are a part. A lot of James' letter is saying, "Because most of the way you think is based off of the way of life in your old culture, this is naturally how you are inclined to think and live. This is how your mind automatically thinks. But there is another way of life. It is the culture in which God's kingdom operates. This is the way God designed for us to think and live."

James' letter is very disorienting. He confronts our cultural blind spots by revealing to us the perspective and design that God has for our life. James wrote his letter to people who already knew and believed the gospel. Jesus wrote his letter to say, "In light of the victory that King Jesus has won, this is how you are to live as citizens of the Kingdom of God. You are to live your life in light of the victory that Christ has won." James does not explicitly spell out the gospel in his letter. A large part of why he does this is intentional. James does not explicitly talk about Jesus and what he has done because his letter is intended to drive us back to our need for the gospel. When we are confronted with the teaching James presents, it becomes evident that we cannot live it out in our own strength. We will only live under the rule of King Jesus to the degree that we understand and are grateful for what he has done to bring us into his Kingdom.

James' lack of explicit teaching about the gospel does not in any way minimize our need to know, believe and rest in what Christ has accomplished for us through his life, death and resurrection. We must always seek to stay centered on the gospel. James does not explicitly talk about the gospel, but this does not in any way go against our need to stay centered on the gospel. James' letter reminds us that grace is always soaked in sweat. True grace always results in obedience. Contrasting grace with obedience is like contrasting a cucumber with a cucumber plant. Cucumber plants always produce cucumbers. People who are citizens of God's Kingdom will live like citizens of God's Kingdom. This does not mean that we never forget of whose Kingdom we are a part. But it does mean that the way we live shows of which Kingdom we are a citizen. It is the tendency of the human heart to manufacture fake fruit. Self-righteousness is a temptation we always will face on some level. But this does not change the fact that grace always produces obedience. We work *out* what God works *in* to us. If we are not working out our faith in obedience, it is because God's grace is not being worked into our heart. When God implants new life into us, the result is new living. Our obedience does not make us a citizen of God's Kingdom any more than taping cucumbers on a tomato plant makes that plant a cucumber plant. But our citizenship does result in us coming to live like citizens of the Kingdom of which we are a part.

James' letter is painfully practical. James knows the human heart very well. He knows how easy it is to get off track. His letter is a map that shows us the path we need to walk. His letter is a pair of glasses that allow us to see the path where God has put us. His letter provides the boots we need to walk on that path. James is inviting us to live in light of the victory Christ has already won. He is teaching us how to live as the citizens we already are. May this book immerse you into what life is like in God's Kingdom!

Rise to the Occasion
(James 1:1)

"And at that time there was a great persecution against the church which was at Jerusalem; and they were all scattered abroad throughout the regions of Judaea and Samaria, except the apostles." Acts 8:1bc

Every word of Scripture is inspired by God. The very words of Scripture are the very words of God. And every word is important. Even something that seems as simple and insignificant as an introduction is useful to study and know. God can speak to us powerfully through what seems to be a section or verse of Scripture we might be tempted to skip over so that we can get to the "good stuff." God speaks through all of Scripture, if we are open to hearing from him.

According to church tradition, this letter was written by James, the half-brother of Jesus. What is interesting about this is how James introduces himself. James could have said, "James, the half-brother of Jesus." James could have also said, "James, the elder of the Jerusalem Church." There are a lot of legitimate ways that James could have identified himself. Instead of boasting of the blessings and privileges he had been given, James boasts of the highest privilege he had: being "a servant of God and of the Lord Jesus Christ." James knew that his identity and role was not primarily as Jesus' half-brother or as an elder. James knew that he had been saved by God's grace for the purpose of serving to advance God's kingdom. James knew that his task was to serve and to teach others how to serve God's kingdom. He does not lift himself above the people to whom he is writing. He humbly states that he is a servant. He is aiming to get the people who received this letter to follow his example.

One thing about James not mentioning being Jesus' half-brother is that it implies that Jesus was no mere human. Jesus was human in every way that we are, but he is also in every way God. Jesus is Lord. Jesus is not just James' half-brother; he is also James' Lord. James recognizes that Jesus has authority over his life. James gladly serves King Jesus.

Who was James writing to? James was writing to 'the twelve tribes in the Dispersion." This letter was very likely written before the year A.D. 48, which means it was probably written before the Jerusalem Council (see Acts 15).The Jerusalem Council was when the Church got together to figure out what God required of non-Jewish believers who wished to join the Church. Non-Jewish believers were not part of the Church until that time, as the message about the Messiah was supposed to first go to people of Jewish descent before it was to be told to people who were not Jewish. James was probably writing to Jewish Christians who had been scattered throughout the area outside of Jerusalem due to persecution. James was a leader of the church that was in Jerusalem. With many of his church members scattered about, he probably felt the need to write to them to instruct them on how they should live. Because they already had a foundation of who Jesus is and what he did, James set out to instruct them about how they could best put their faith into action.

One of the things the phrase "the twelve tribes which are scattered abroad" would have brought to mind in the people to whom he was writing would be the times in Israel's past when they were exiled out of their land. By using this phrase, James would be letting them know, "I know you are suffering. I know you are being persecuted. I know you are facing trials. I know it is difficult to accept the fact that the people who are persecuting you used to be your spiritual leaders. I know these people used to be your friends and family. I know you are trying to piece all of these things together. I know this is not easy for you."

Another thing this phrase would have brought to mind is the fact that they are the true people of God—unlike the people who were persecuting them in God's name. In ancient Israel, there were twelve tribes that made up the people of Israel. James was using this phrase to say, "You are the true Israel. You are the true people of God. The promises of God have been fulfilled through Jesus and you are partaking of that. You are the ones who will inherit God's kingdom. Do not be afraid. God will vindicate you. Press on in your faith. Keep on keeping on and don't let anything stop you."

James addresses his audience by referring to himself in a term that models who they are to be and how they are to live. James takes the initiative to lead his people by example. James not only leads his people by example, he also lets them know he is aware of all of the trouble and hardship they are going through. James also introduces his letter by encouraging them to remember that they are the true people of God and that they will inherit the promises of God. James points them back to times past when God had proven his faithfulness to his people. James points them back to times past to remind them that God was faithful back then and is still faithful today. It is in this context that James writes this letter.

Joy in the Midst of Trials
(James 1:2-4)

Life is a series of complex and often contrasting experiences. We experience moments of pure ecstasy and moments of profound sorrow. While we do experience innumerable good things throughout our day, the reality is that we live in a world of joy interrupted. Trials come into our life. Trials come to us every day. Sometimes the trials are minor: heavy traffic on the way to work; a neighbor who never seems to be able to mind their own business; our favorite shirt getting ruined in the wash. Sometimes the trials are major: the death of a child; the loss of a job; a debilitating illness. Whether the trials we face are minor or major, we all face trials. We will face lots of trials over the course of our life.

The typical way we see trials are as purposeless potholes in the road of life. We see trials as something we just have to endure and get through the best way we know how. But God desires for us to view our trials in an altogether different way. God desires that we view the trials that come to us as purposeful perfectors of our faith. Trials sift us. Trials cause us to respond in ways that reveal what we are really trusting in. Trials reveal what we are building our lives upon. Trials reveal what we are really worshipping in our daily lives. They reveal what we are made of when the rubber must meet the road.

When trials come we should ask ourselves, "What is God showing me through this trial? What is this trial exposing in my heart? What does my reaction to this trial show that I have been building my life upon?" Trials present us with a choice. How we

16

respond will make us either wiser or it will darken our heart, but it will not leave us the same. How we respond to trials will make us either better or bitter, but it will not leave us the same as we were before. Trials provide us with the opportunity to know God more intimately and to trust him more fully. Difficulties and trials force us to realize that we need God more than we have ever realized before. Trials help us to know that our deepest, most abiding need is God.

Trials are going to come into our life. We can have joy in the midst of trials when we know that God is at work to wean us off of trusting in anything other than in him. We can have joy in the midst of trials because we know that while the trial itself is not something to rejoice about, we can rejoice in the fact that God is at work to move our heart to a place where we will be more satisfied in all of who he is for us. We have the freedom to let God do his work in the midst of our trials because we know that what God is doing is moving us to a place where our joy can increase and overflow.

Wisdom is a Person (James 1:5-8)

"...Christ the power of God, and the wisdom of God." 1 Corinthians 1:24

Additional Reading: Proverbs 3:5-8; Colossians 2:1-3

Infidelity. Divorce. Cancer. Infertility. The unexpected death of a loved one. Loss of a job. An estranged son or daughter. Marital strife. Miscarriage. A debilitating disease. Few things are able to break through our delusion of self-sufficiency like the trials that come into our lives; trials that show us we don't have the resources needed to solve the problem; trials that crush us and reveal how helpless we truly are. It is during times like these that we see most clearly our greatest need.

During times like these our greatest need is not for information or knowledge about how to deal with the trial in front of us. Our greatest need is for God. We need a God who will help us make sense of the situation. We need a God who will meet us right where we are, in the midst of our brokenness and mess. We need a God who will walk with us; a God who will carry us when we do not have the strength to go any further. The wisdom we need to help get us through trials is not some type of abstract philosophy to help us figure out how to fix our life. The wisdom we need is a Person. The wisdom we need is the Person of Jesus Christ.

Jesus Christ most fully shows us who God is and what God is like. Jesus reveals the grace and mercy that God desires to extend to us. The wisdom of every worldview other than Christianity involves man reaching up to heaven; it is about man ascending to a plane higher than the current one. But in Christianity, heaven comes down to man, extending to us love, grace and mercy beyond anything we could ever imagine. The wisdom we need to deal with the trials that come into our life comes out of the place of knowing our need for God and knowing that God will meet those who come to him in childlike dependence and trust. Because of Christ we can come to God--and keep coming to God--knowing that he will never turn us away. The way to God and the way he designed us to live comes to us through Jesus, who is the Wisdom and Power of God.

When You Don't Know, Ask
(James 1:5-8)

At its root, wisdom is not abstract principles or a philosophy for living. Wisdom is a Person. The sum and essence of wisdom is Jesus Christ. But what do we do when we don't even know how to begin to handle the circumstances in front of us? What should we do when we need to deal with problems to which we can't find a solution? What should we do when we don't know what to do? Wisdom is a Person, but how does this help us on a practical level?

First, we must admit our need for God's help. If we do not see our need for help (or if we are too proud to admit that we need help), God will likely not give us the wisdom we need. People who do not think they need help will not ask for it. People who do not want to be helped will not accept help if it happens to come their way. If we see that we need God's help and are willing to admit it, we will ask God for the help we need.

Second, we must ask God for help. We must ask God to give us the wisdom for how to best deal with the troubling situation. It sounds simple, but we often do not receive the help we need because we do not ask for it. Relationships are built on communication. Communication is the glue that holds relationships together. If there is no communication, then there is no functional relationship. God desires for us to communicate with him.

Not only do we need to ask, we must remember *how* God gives to those who ask. God gives *generously* to all who ask him. God is not a begrudging Father. Jesus said, "If ye then, being evil,

20

know how to give good gifts unto your children, how much more shall your Father which is in heaven give good things to them that ask him?"(Matthew 7:11). God delights in giving us good things. Wisdom is a good thing that God will give to us every time we ask for it. Knowing *how* God gives to us is important because it plays into how we must ask if we are going to receive anything from him. We are to ask God in faith. Why is it important that we ask God in faith for wisdom? Faith has to do with God's goodness. Faith has to do not only with believing in God's existence, it also has to do with believing in God's goodness. God "is a rewarder of them that diligently seek him" (Hebrews 11:6).

One of the implications of asking God in faith for wisdom is that it means we believe God will answer us. Which means that when we ask, we must be willing to act on whatever answers God gives us. Before God tells us what to do, we should already have our mind made up that we are going to act on what he will tell us to do. If we view the wisdom of God as one of many options for how to handle the problem we are facing, God is not going to speak to us. But if we know that the wisdom God desires to give us will be the best possible solution, he will give us exactly what we need. God will answer us above and beyond anything we could have hoped. In what problem areas of your life are you most prone to try to solve apart from God's wisdom? What keeps you from asking God for the wisdom you need?

Living Right Side Up in an Upside Down World (James 1:9-11)

Additional Reading: Jeremiah 9:23-24; Matthew 6:19-24

Few roads spark my interest like Stratford Road in Winston-Salem, North Carolina, does; especially the part of Stratford Road that goes through Buena Vista, a wealthy section of the city. Few roads allure me and lead me to envy like Stratford Road does either. A drive through Buena Vista any time of the day almost always results in seeing some type of nice, shiny, expensive sports car—the type of sports cars guys put up posters of in their garage. The type of sports cars that scream of power—power under the hood, and powerful enough to attract the most beautiful women around. Sometimes when I see one of these sports cars on Stratford Road I get lost in a daydream about me driving the car down the road with a beautiful woman sitting next to me in the passenger seat.

I usually come out of my daydreams to the harsh realization that I am, in fact, not in a sports car, but in a Buick that is over 15 years old. It is a Buick some of my friends lovingly refer to as "the Boat" or "Grandpa's Power House." But after this harsh realization sets in, I usually remember that any woman who would want me for my car would only be interested in me for my money. She may be a beautiful gold-digger, but a gold-digger nonetheless. Truth be told, if I had a sports car it probably would not take long before I lost my license for having too many speeding tickets. So I stumble out of my daydream with the realization that desiring "the good life" can cost us more than it is worth in the long run.

The temptations that come with "the good life" can be overwhelming. "The good life" can cause us to lose perspective. So much so, that we may be living our lives walking the road of life on a path made of eggshell dreams—ones that may crush under our feet more easily than we will admit. The scary thing is that we can see the world in a way that is upside-down for so long we no longer know which way is up.

God's kingdom is set up in a way that is completely backwards from the way this world operates. Our world is set up on the principle where having wealth and power is the key to a good life. "He who dies with the most toys wins," or so we are led to believe. But in reality, the person who is lowly is actually the one who has the advantage. Wealth and power are not inherently evil. These two things can be excellent tools we use to accomplish much good. But wealth and power always have an inherent danger that comes with them. Wealth and power can easily give us the illusion that we are much more self-sufficient than we actually are; we can trust more in our wealth and power than we trust in God—and we can be completely oblivious that this is, in fact, going on in our heart.

Not only can wealth and power give us the illusion that we are self-sufficient, they are also a danger because they can distract us from the things that really matter. We can become so preoccupied with what we touch and see that we become blind to the fact that these things will not last forever. Wealth and power can only be used properly when we view them in light of eternity. We cannot keep wealth and power forever. There is no certainty in them. At best,

23

we can keep them until the day we die. But the fact of the matter is that we will die. It could happen at any time. In and of themselves, wealth and power provide no lasting meaning for our life. They are as fleeting as snow that falls in the middle of spring: here only for a brief moment and then gone.

The rich in this world are those who have at least some level of self-sufficiency. The rich in this world are not an elite class of people; they are people who have some way of helping themselves. Lest we be naïve, it is almost always the case that we possess far more wealth and power than we realize or are willing to admit. The lowly have good reason to praise God in that they do not have as many distractions and hindrances to keep them from focusing their heart toward God. The rich in this world should pray for protection from falling into the snare that wealth and power can be. The rich in this world should pray that God helps them to see through the alluring deception that wealth and power can have over us. The rich in this world should pray that their eyes will be opened to the fleeting nature of wealth and power. The rich in this world should pray for the wisdom to know how to use their resources properly. What God desires is not that we would have freedom from wealth and power, but that we would have freedom from being ensnared by the alluring deception that accompanies wealth and power. May God help us to view the things he has given to us in light of eternity!

The Temptation of Blessings
(James 1:9-12)

The adversities that come into our life are not the only trials we face. Success and prosperity are also trials that are part of life. <u>How we respond to the success and prosperity that comes into our life is a good indicator of what our heart really trusts.</u> How we respond to the success and prosperity we experience reveals that upon which we are building our life. There are several questions we can ask ourselves to measure where our heart is.

When I am given authority, how do I use it? Do I use it for personal gain or for the greater good of what I have been given authority over? *How am I at work ???*

What might the people I have authority over say about me and the way I use my authority?

How do I spend my money when I have excess?

What am I spending my money on now?

Is the car I have something I chose for functional purposes or did I choose it for some other reason (comfort, status symbol, etc)?

How do I use my home? Do I view my home as something that exists primarily for my comfort and pleasure or do I view my home as something I have been given to bless others with? Do I invite other people into my home?

This I want to do

Thank you Father for this home you have given my family.

25

How we answer these questions gives us a good idea for what we are truly living. Success and prosperity do not change us. Success and prosperity merely bring out who we really are. How we respond to success and prosperity will either make us wiser, or it will darken our heart. The one thing it won't do is leave us the same as before. We will either gain perspective or lose perspective through how we respond. Our experiences shape us and mold us into the person we are. Our experiences set the course for where we are going in life. When success and prosperity come into our life we should praise God for it. And we should ask God to make us aware of what is going on in our heart. We should ask God to give us the wisdom and purity of heart to make us good stewards of his gifts. May God make us aware of the trials that come to us in beautiful packages!

Walk with the End in Mind
(James 1:12)

I am an Eagle Scout. Growing up, I spent many weekends and school holidays on camping trips. On most of these trips we went hiking. Some of my fondest memories are of the trips I went on as a Boy Scout. While I had a lot of fun on these hiking trips, I also very clearly remember how intensely difficult some of these trips were. There were trips where we had to hike over difficult terrain. Sometimes we would have to hike several miles up very steep inclines.

I remember one hiking trip where I did not know if I could keep hiking. We had been hiking uphill on a steep incline for around three hours. Several of the boys, myself included, had twisted our ankles on many of the jagged rocks that were all over the trail. There was no good place on the trail to put our feet. Every step of the trail was uncomfortable. And after having to carefully maneuver our feet for several hours, hiking became very painful, exhausting and frustrating. There were very few safe places where we could stop and rest along the way. Needless to say, all of the Scouts complained most of the way to the top. The more we complained, the more our leaders told us about the spectacular view at the top of the mountain. Only one of the Scouts had ever been to the top of the mountain. He was the only one who didn't complain during this treacherous hike. The hike was so relentless that it became difficult to even conceive it would be well worth it when we got to the top.

After a long, grueling four hours of hiking uphill we finally made it. Never in my entire life had I been somewhere that beautiful. When we reached the top of the mountain, all of our pain, difficulties and exhaustion seemed to be a small price to pay for such an awesome view. When I saw the top of the mountain and the view it gave, it was almost as if I completely forgot about the pain in my legs and feet. I was lost and in awe of the beauty before me. If I had known about the beauty awaiting us, I would not have complained and lost sight of where we were going.

We hiked this trail several times in the years of Scouting that followed. Every time we took someone with us who had never been, they could not understand why some of us were hiking such a difficult trail with so much joy. They did not know that our joy came from knowing where we were going. We were hiking the same grueling path they were, but we did it with joy because our eyes were fixed on the destination we were walking toward.

Our spiritual life is a lot like this story. We are on a trail leading somewhere that is better than we could ever imagine. We have not been there yet, so we don't quite know what to expect. We cannot see our destination. All that we see is the difficult path ahead of us. We get distracted along the way. We sometimes focus so much on trying to find a comfortable place to rest that we lose sight of our destination. Our hike becomes focused more on alleviating our pain and finding comfort than it is on ensuring that we make it to the top of the mountain. Taking time to recover and rest is important, but it is not an end in itself. The purpose of taking time to rest and recover is so we'll have the strength to continue hiking toward the destination.

Distractions are inevitable while hiking our trail. Distractions come to us in two forms. One form of distraction is trials. Trials take our eyes off our destination. They cause us to focus on our pain and exhaustion rather than on making it to the top of the mountain. It is much more difficult to continue on God's path for us when we focus on anything other than where we are going. Yes, it is painful when we lose our job or experience a pay cut. Yes, it is painful when there is conflict between us and the people we love. Yes, our body starts to get weak and deteriorate as we walk along the path. Sometimes the path God has placed us on is not anything like what we had imagined or hoped it would be. Sometimes there are moments in life when we would rather lie down on the side of the trail and die than get back up and keep walking. But the only way we are going to be able to have the strength and perspective to keep putting one foot in front of the other is by remembering and focusing on where it is we are headed. In heaven, we will have no more pain and no more sickness. There will be no more death. God will wipe away every tear from our eyes. We have to remind ourselves that the pain, discomfort and loss we are experiencing right now is temporary and that we are headed for a glorious future that is far better than anything we can even imagine.

Another form of distraction comes from good things. Honestly, if there had been fun places to stop along the path on that Scout trip, we probably never would have made it to the top of the mountain. If there had been a nice, grassy area to rest and play in, we might have wasted a lot of time and would not have been able to make it to the top of the mountain before dark. If there had been a pool of fresh water in which we could've gone swimming, we might have been tempted to trade the beauty of the mountaintop for a few hours in an ordinary body of water. There would not have been anything wrong with doing either of these things. Those are good, fun things to do. But the temptation that comes with good, fun things is that if we let them distract us from getting to our destination, we will not make it to the top of the mountain. And the beauty at the top of the mountain is far better than anything we could do along the way. Yes, your spouse is a wonderful gift from God. Yes, your children are wonderful gifts from God. Your ability to make money is a gift from God. Your job is a gift from God. Your car is a gift from God. Your house is a gift from God. Going to the beach is a gift from God. These are all good things. But the satisfaction they bring us is only temporary. These things are like signposts that are meant to point us to the mountaintop. They are not the destination. When we let good things distract us, it is like camping out at the signposts. The signposts are good, but they are not the mountaintop. We were made for the mountaintop. Anything less than the mountaintop will eventually strip us of our humanity and leave us broken and alone on the side of the mountain. We cannot let good things distract us from getting to the mountaintop. We can enjoy the good things that God gives us along the way, but we cannot let these good things consume the affections of our heart.

We were made for God. We were made for eternity. The difficulties, trials, successes, failures and good things that we have in this life are temporary. They do not last forever. God has put us on a path meant to lead us to heaven. The only way we will not be distracted by things behind us or ahead of us on the trail is to keep our eyes on where we are going. Though the path feels difficult and confusing, and though sometimes we get distracted by signposts provided to guide us, we are headed for the top of the mountain. We have never been there, but Jesus has gone there before us. He has cleared the trail and has left the Holy Spirit to guide us along in our journey. If we listen we will hear his voice calling to us from the top of the mountain. The path is not easy. There will be temptations that are calling us to give up and leave the trail for other pursuits. But if we will listen to the voice of Jesus that is calling out to us from the mountaintop, the more we keep walking and the closer we get to the top of the mountain, the louder and sweeter his voice becomes. And the louder his voice becomes, the more real the mountaintop will become to us. With each step of faith, we are getting closer and closer to the top of the mountain.

The Blame Game (James 1:12-14)

Additional Reading: Genesis 3:8-12

"If God hadn't given me such a stubborn spouse,
I wouldn't have to be so harsh in getting him to listen
to me."

"God has given me such a great job. I know the hours
are keeping me away from my family and church most
of the time, but this job is such a blessing to me. I can
finally have the lifestyle I've always wanted."

"God knows I have an addictive personality. He
understands that I'm prone to fall back into drinking
too much when I am out with my friends."

"It's only pornography. I'm not really cheating on my
wife. God gave us our sexuality. I have to have some
way to deal with it. Since my spouse won't have sex
with me as much as I want to, I have to have some
way to deal with my urges. It is natural."

Two things that go hand in hand with sin are
shirking responsibility and blame-shifting. Sin causes
us to find reasons to justify the things we do. Instead
of taking responsibility for our actions, we try to shift
the blame off ourselves. We blame our circumstances
for why we do the things we do. We attribute the real
problem to something that is outside of ourselves. We
pretend that our sin is not our own fault.

Although we usually don't consciously think of
blame-shifting this way, every time we shift the blame

for our sin off ourselves we are actually blaming God for it. Blaming and questioning God often happens explicitly during times when we lose something important to us. Although we don't usually explicitly blame God for our sin, every time we try to justify our sin we are pointing our finger at God; we are making God out to be the one who is responsible for our sin.

Our circumstances are not the deepest problem in our life. God cannot be blamed for why we sin. The deepest problem we have in life does not exist outside ourselves. In fact, the vast majority of the problems we face have very little to do with anything that exists beyond ourselves. Our deepest, most pervasive problem is our desire, and the heart from which our desires flow. The most destructive force at work in our life is our own heart. Our thoughts, words and choices are governed by our heart; they are controlled and mastered by what is in our heart.

Although our sin causes us to want to shift the blame off ourselves, not taking responsibility for our sin is the worst thing we can do. "There is a way that seemeth right unto a man, but the end thereof are the ways of death" (Proverbs 16:25). Instead of trying to shift the blame for our sin off ourselves, we should confess our sin to God. God will freely pardon all who confess their sin to him; God will freely pardon and accept all who come to him with repentance and faith. Denial will not ease the cancer of sin that eats away at our soul. Face your sin head-on by confessing it to God and you will find the healing and wholeness you so desperately need.

How God Defines Freedom
(James 1:13-15)

Additional Reading: John 8:34-36

Sin is like a disease. When it comes to the nature of sin, our words and actions are like coughing is to emphysema. Our words and actions are merely symptoms that show the disease is present. We are sinners not because we sin; we sin because we *are* sinners. The problem is who we are. When Scripture says we are born as sinners it means that down at the very core of who we are, we are sinful. Think of an apple tree. Apple trees produce apples because that is the type tree that is at its roots. An apple tree will never produce peaches because peaches come from peach trees. This is a principle known as organic consistency; things produce according to their kind. This principle is true in the spiritual realm as well. Everything our life produces is the result of who and what we are; what we say and do is controlled and directed by our heart. This is why Scripture calls sin slavery.

We freely make choices; we are the ones who are in control. We are responsible for what we do; no one else can be blamed for what we do. While we are both free to choose whatsoever we want to and are responsible for our choices, we are not born into this world free. Our will is in bondage. We are born free to do anything we desire to do. But what we desire comes out of a heart that is corrupt; we are born into this world with a sinful nature we inherited from Adam, the first human (Romans 5:12-21). We love darkness and hate the light (John 3:19-20). We are hostile to

34

God (Romans 8:7). We do not seek God apart from him drawing us to himself (Romans 3:11; John 6:44). We don't want to accept the truth; we refuse to acknowledge the truth (Romans 1:18-32). We are blind to the truth because of the hardness of our hearts; we cannot see the truth because we are unwilling to see the truth (Ephesians 4:18). We are spiritual "Helen Kellers"; we cannot see the truth (Isaiah 59:10; 1 Corinthians 2:14; 2 Corinthians 4:4). We are dead in our sins (Ephesians 2:1; Colossians 2:13). So while we make all of our choices freely and voluntarily, we are also enslaved and unable to free ourselves from our sin.

We are not able to turn away from our sin. We are captive to sin, self and the devil. We are powerless to do anything to break free from our captivity. We do not need an opportunity to receive salvation. What we need is to be rescued and delivered. We need grace that is able to soften our hard hearts. We need grace that is actually able to overcome our stubborn and rebellious heart. We need more than God offering us salvation — we need God to step in and save us. We need grace that is sovereign. We need grace that will overtake and overcome our hearts.

Our sin problem is much deeper than we would ever admit, had God not told us in Scripture. We often miss out on knowing the full depth of God's love and grace because we are too proud to accept the truth about how helpless and powerless we are over our sin. The degree to which we reject the truth about how depraved we are is the degree to which we have contempt for the grace of God. The degree to which we soften the truth about our utter powerlessness over our sin is the degree to which we lessen our experience of the grace of God.

Don't miss out on knowing the full depth of God's grace because you refuse to see yourself as Scripture reveals you were before he saved you. Don't miss out on knowing the full depth of God's grace because you want to believe you have self-sovereignty over your salvation. Don't rob yourself of the opportunity to rejoice in the great salvation that God has given to you. Accept who God says you used to be. Accept how utterly helpless and lost you were. Accept how enslaved you were. When you do, you will find a depth to the grace of God far beyond anything you can fathom. You will find grace to be the most amazing thing in the universe.

The Path that Leads to Death (James 1:14-15)

Additional Reading: Ephesians 4:17-24; Psalm 32:8-11

There is a process that happens inside us every time we sin. There are steps that precede our sin; steps that lead us into sin. Sin always starts with a desire in our heart. Our soul is filled with longing for something we know we shouldn't have. We are filled with an overwhelming yearning. Our desire becomes so overwhelming we begin to think of what we want. We begin to fix our attention on this desire. And then we begin to make a plan that allows us to fulfill our desire. After we have figured out how we are going to satisfy our desire, we start to put our plan into action.

Once we choose to entertain a sinful desire with our mind and we begin to dwell on it, we have already fallen into sin. Once we have fixed our gaze upon the thing that we desire, more often than not we are already past the point of no return; we will carry out fulfilling that desire. This is why sin is so dangerous. Sin always gives birth to death. "For the wages of sin is death" (Romans 6:23a).

God set up the world to operate on the principle of justice. This means that what we sow, we will reap. Sometimes we do encounter trouble through no fault of our own. We live in a broken world. Sometimes we reap the effects of something we did not sow. While this is true, it is also equally true that we cannot escape the consequences of our actions. We cannot sow bad seeds and reap a good harvest. It cannot happen. We were made to glorify God and enjoy him forever. Anything we do that does not

37

involve us glorifying and enjoying God is completely foreign to who we were made to be and what we were made to do. When we do not live our life for the purpose of glorifying and enjoying God, we are like fish who are trying to live on land rather than in water. It is damaging to us at the most fundamental level. It goes against the deepest part of who we are. It is also offensive to God because it makes a mess out of all the good things he has given us. When we sow the seeds of sin into the garden of our life, we will reap a harvest of death and destruction.

We have to be careful to examine the desires of our heart. Desire in and of itself is neither good nor bad. It is neutral. We were made to desire and long after God. Having desires and longings is a fundamental part of who we are. The problem is not desire. The problem is when we have the wrong type of desire. Our desires are deceitful when we are ignorant of the truth. We are born into this world in a state of total spiritual blindness; we are ignorant of the truth. Our ignorance and blindness are due to the hardness of our heart.

The good news is that when God opened our eyes to the truth of the gospel, he also gave us a new heart. God gave us a heart that is pliable and open to receiving the truth. God gave us a heart that is open to correction. God gave us a heart that allows us to truly be able to change. God gave us a heart that can understand and respond to the truth.

This means that we can break away from our old way of life. We can break free from sowing seeds of sin into the garden of our life. We are free from having to making choices that will lead us into death and destruction. We have a heart that will produce life when it has been informed and saturated with the truth. We have a heart that desires the things of God; we have a heart that loves the things God loves and hates the things God hates. We have freedom. Before God stepped in and rescued us from ourselves, everything we sowed was contributing to our own ruin. But now that God has rescued us he has given us the power to sow seeds into our life that can produce life. Before God rescued us we were leading ourselves one step closer to self-destruction with every choice we made. But now that God has rescued us, we can sow seeds that lead us even further into that which is truly life.

The life we step into grows and grows; it becomes more abundant. God loves his children so much that he not only gives us the freedom to choose, he also gives us the freedom we so desperately need: freedom from sin. We have been given the most precious freedom in the universe. Cherish it.

How Deep Does Grace Go?
(James 1:16-17)

Additional Reading: 1 Corinthians 4:7

It is all too easy to fall into the trap of thinking that we are much more self-sufficient than we actually are. It is easy to believe we are the reason for all of the good things in our life. We tell ourselves, "I've worked hard. I earned it." Yet we overlook the fact that everything we used to "earn" the things we have are themselves gifts from God. Why do your hands and arms move? Why do you have legs that allow you to walk? Where did you get your intelligence? Where did you get your natural abilities? Why were you born with eyes that can see? Why do you deserve the oxygen that comes into your lungs every time you take a breath? What did you do to deserve it?

It is not that we are worms. We are amazing, wonderful creations of God. All human beings have been made in the image of God; we are unique and distinct from every other creature; we have been made to reflect who God is by ruling and reigning over the earth. All human beings have inherent worth and deserve to be treated with dignity. We are truly amazing and wonderful.

The issue is not whether or not we are wonderful creations of God who are capable of doing all types of amazing things. The issue is *why* we are so wonderful and *why* we have the good things that we have. The reason for these two things is God. God is a God of blessing. Though we have done nothing to deserve his favor, he desires to bless us. He has blessed us so much already. It is easy to overlook just how good he is to us. James 1:13-17 is telling us, "Humans are the reason why the world is broken. God cannot be blamed. God is good. He is a blesser. Every good thing we have is because of how good God is. Don't deceive yourself. The evidence of God's goodness is all around you. Don't let pride rob you of knowing how good God is and how much he loves you. Embrace his goodness. His goodness is all around you."

How God Brings Life out of Death (James 1:16-18)

Additional Reading: 2 Corinthians 4:6; John 11:38-44

Falling in love is both a wonderful and terrifying experience. Falling in love is something we have no control over. It is something that seems to overcome and overtake us. Yet it is also something that doesn't happen against our will. Salvation happens to us much in the same way. We must choose to receive Christ; we must choose to turn away from our sin and believe the gospel. Yet it is also something that sort of just happens to us. One moment we are blind to the truth and the next moment we see. One moment the gospel seems like foolishness to us and the next moment the light switch comes on inside our soul and we see the gospel as the most precious reality in the entire universe. We find ourselves in awe of the beauty of who God is and the great love he has for us. Receiving Christ is not less than a choice—but it is certainly much more than a choice. Before a person receives Christ, a miraculous, supernatural awakening has to occur within. Scripture describes this awakening in various ways, some of which include: the new birth, regeneration, being born again and being born from above. James 1:18 gives us some insight into the nature of this awakening. The first thing about this new birth that we must know is that we do not have any control over it. John 1:13 tells us we become children of God not because of our physical birth, nor because of anything we do, nor because of any decision we make. We become children of God because God supernaturally gives us

42

the new birth; we are children of God "of HIS own will" (James 1:18). We have no more control over our new birth than we had over our own physical birth. When children are angry at their parents they sometimes say, "I didn't ask to be born." They say that as a way to blame their parents for whatever hardship they are dealing with. We know that we do not cause our own birth, which is one reason why Scripture refers to it as a new birth. We can no more contribute to becoming alive spiritually than a dead person contributes to coming back to life. This is really great news. If the new birth were ultimately up to us it would never happen. Because we come into this world spiritually dead, our new birth being "of [God's] own will" is our only hope. We have been corrupted by sin down to our very roots. Apart from God intervening and changing our heart, we would never choose to receive Christ.

The second thing we need to know is how the new birth happens. God "begat...us with the word of truth." What does this mean? It means that we heard the gospel. And it means that we *heard* the gospel. Through the preaching of the gospel, God calls us to himself. There are two main types of callings God gives when we hear the gospel. One calling is an outward calling. It is the invitation to turn away from our sin and believe the gospel. Everyone who hears the gospel receives this call from God. The second type of calling is an inward calling. Theologians sometimes refer to this as "effectual calling." It is a calling that affects a response in us.

This type of calling is illustrated for us in John 11:38-44 where Jesus raises Lazarus from the dead. Jesus calls Lazarus *by name* and tells him to come out of the grave. Jesus' call brought about Lazarus being raised to life. It happens like falling in love does: Lazarus had no control over it AND it did not happen against his will. There was no collaborative effort happening between Jesus and Lazarus to bring Lazarus back to life. Lazarus had nothing to do with it. At the same time, Lazarus willingly and freely responded to Jesus' call. This same type of calling happened when God created the heavens and the earth. When God said "Let there be light," light leapt into existence at the command of his word. His calling brought about what we said.

Through the gospel, God the Holy Spirit calls people by name with this type of calling. This calling evokes a response in us. Just as Lazarus responded to Jesus' calling, we too respond to the gospel in the exact same way. It is an instantaneous reaction where God quickens us out of our spiritual deadness and we respond to that quickening with faith. The new birth and our faith happen together. Faith is the evidence we are born again, not the cause. Faith is not something we contribute in the sense that faith comes from us. Faith is produced in our hearts by God the Holy Spirit through God's word when it is being proclaimed through the power of the Holy Spirit. Faith itself is a gift from God. The faith with which we believe the gospel is only our own because God gave it to us by supernaturally imparting it into our heart.

Yes, we chose. Yes, we chose freely. Yes, we decided to follow Jesus. No one did that for us and we cannot be saved without doing it. But the reason we chose to receive Christ is in itself due to the goodness and grace of God. Everything about our salvation— even our decision—finds its origin in the grace of God that has rescued us from the course we had set for our self-destruction. There is no limit to how far God's grace is able to reach out and save us. This is the best news of all: grace has no conditions. Grace meets every single requirement we need in order to know God and be brought back to him. There is a grace that goes deeper than we can know on the level with which we experience it. Don't miss the depth of his great grace and love for you.

Anger is Always about a Kingdom (James 1:19-20)

Additional Reading: Jeremiah 2:9-13; Matthew 5:6

I do not remember what I said, but I will never forget the look on his face. My words cut him deeply, like a switchblade knife pulled out quickly and unexpectedly stuck in his gut. The words just jumped out of my mouth. In a flash of anger I lashed out with my words. Words I could never take back. Words that I'm sure he will never forget.

I learned that day just how powerful our words can be. I wish I could say that day was a turning point for me; that I learned to be more careful with my words; that I never hurt another person with my words. The truth is that while my immediate response to that situation was grief and sorrow, very little changed in the months that followed. While I knew my words created problems in my life, I didn't know or understand why I said the things I said. It wasn't until much later that I saw the reason we say the things we say.

Why are we so slow to listen, so quick to speak and so quick to become angry? And why is it so difficult for us to be quick to listen, slow to speak and slow to become angry? The answer to these two questions might surprise us. The answer to these two questions doesn't have anything to do with our words at all. The reason we respond to other people the way we do is because of the kingdom we are living for. Many theologians have claimed that the most-central concept in all of Scripture is the concept of a kingdom. In Scripture, the kingdom of God is not a place. The

46

kingdom of God is the reign and rule of God over something. Therefore, a kingdom is what has sway over our heart; a kingdom is where we center our lives. A kingdom is what guides and directs all we say and do.

There is a reason we are often slow to listen, quick to speak and quick to become angry. The reason is because we are living for our own kingdom; we are living for our own claustrophobic kingdom centered on ourselves. We are the ruler of our kingdom. We decide the rules; we decide the way things are; we decide how things should be. We want life to be our way. We don't want to consider what other people have to say because we already know how we think things are or should be. We are more interested in being heard than we are about saying what would be most helpful for the situation at hand. After all, we assume, if we can just get them to listen to what we have to say they will realize how brilliant our ideas are.

We get angry when other people violate the rules of our kingdom. Anger in and of itself is not wrong. Rather, what is wrong is almost always the reason why we get angry. Most of our anger is a response to something that is getting in the way of our kingdom; most of the time our anger has nothing to do with God's kingdom. Anger rooted in our own selfishness cannot produce the righteousness of God.

The righteousness of God is not primarily ethical or moral in nature. It is also about much more than obeying God from our heart. The righteousness of God is fundamentally about God's glory. God is righteous because he is unswervingly devoted to his own glory above all other things. God is wholeheartedly devoted to his glory because he alone is worthy and because he alone can satisfy our heart. The righteousness of God is fundamentally about the allegiance of our heart; for whom and what we are living. We were made to glorify God and enjoy him forever. Our happiness and God's glory were made to go hand in hand. Trying to live our life for anything other than the glory of God is foreign to how God has wired us to operate.

The anger, confusion, heartache and miscommunication that plague so much of our relationships are often due to the fact we are devoted to our own kingdom to the point we are more than willing to bring our own life to complete and utter ruin. The choices people make every day prove this. The unraveling of people's lives might happen slowly like the bank of a river eroding with the passing of time. We reap what we sow. "There is a way that seemeth right unto a man, but the end thereof are the ways of death" (Proverbs 16:25). Eventually life catches up with us. We cannot escape this reality. We were made for God. We cannot be whole without him. Our anger tells us something about our heart. Our anger reveals what is really going on inside of us. Our anger reveals the kingdom for which we are truly living. More destructive than our anger are the reasons for our anger.

Pay attention to what makes you angry. Dig beneath the surface and consider the source of your anger; figure out why you are angry. When you feel yourself becoming angry, slow down and pause for a moment to remember God's goodness; slow down to remember that lasting joy can only be found through seeking after God's kingdom. Slow down and weigh your heart. Slow down and consider what you might say that would communicate grace and mercy—the same grace and mercy you yourself are utterly dependent on receiving from God. Slow down and consider what would be the most helpful and beneficial response you can give. Slow down and put aside your agenda. Open your heart and ears to consider what is being said to you. Listen not only to the words being said, but also to the heart and intent behind what they are saying. Doing this opens up doors for effective communication and real intimacy to take place; doing so allows real progress to be made through our interactions.

Not being driven by our own kingdom frees us from a lot of destructive anger and the effect it has on our life. Not being driven by our own kingdom frees us to handle difficult situations in ways that are constructive and more likely to produce positive results. Not being driven by our own kingdom frees us from feeling like we have to have control over things we cannot control.

Living our life with a heart devoted to God's kingdom frees us. It brings us into alignment with whom we were created to be and what we were created to do. The sense of wholeness and satisfaction our hearts so desperately long for is found through acknowledging our selfish anger, forsaking our devotion to our own claustrophobic kingdom, and turning our heart toward Jesus and the kingdom he came to establish.

Fighting From Victory (James 1:21)

Additional Reading: Isaiah 57:15; Matthew 5:29-30;
2nd Corinthians 6:16-7:1

The war raging for the allegiance of our heart must be fought. The devotion we have to our own kingdom is not something that can easily be broken. Sinful human beings are pathologically selfish. Our allegiance to God's kingdom happens only through grace. The more we taste God's goodness, the more free we become to live our life for his glory. However, as people already saved, we are not passive in our growing in grace. James gives us some things we must do if we are to gain victory over the sin in our life.

The first two things James exhorts us to do are to put away or rid ourselves of something. We are told to remove something from ourselves in the way we remove wet or dirty clothes. We need to strip something off ourselves so as to remove it as completely as we can. What we are told to put away is "all filthiness and superfluity of naughtiness."

What is filthiness? Filthiness is something that pollutes or contaminates us outside ourselves. Filthiness is the result of something external that impacts us in a negative way. Like dirt that covers a freshly washed pair of white clothes. The dirt ruins the outfit. What James is telling us is that we need to put away the things that lead us into sin. Movies, music, magazines, places, people; anything that will lead us into temptation we know we cannot resist. We are to remove these things from having a negative influence on our life. Often the best way to do this is to know

50

what our limitations are. For example, if you struggle with drinking too much, it is probably unwise to spend time at bars. If you struggle with lust, you might not want to watch movies you know will lead your heart and mind to places it doesn't need to go. If you struggle with your identity ("Who am I?"), you might want to stay away from magazines that aim at helping you to develop an identity foreign to who God says you are. Just as giving alcohol to an alcoholic only serves to feed their addiction, so, too, surrounding ourselves with things that appeal to our sinful appetites only serves to feed our addiction to self. If we pump garbage into ourselves, we should not be surprised when what comes out is garbage as well. What and whom we surround ourselves with will influence us, for better or for worse.

One thing James is not telling us to do is to separate ourselves from the world. We live in a broken, messed-up world. We cannot get away from all of the wrong things that are in the world. Even if we could do that, James would never tell us to separate ourselves from the world. For it is by living in the midst of our broken, messed-up world that others will be able to come to experience the new life Christ offers them. What James *is* telling us to do is to not let something have so much influence over us that it causes us to stumble. For example, if someone does not struggle with drinking too much, then going to a bar or having a drink with their dinner is not something they necessary need to avoid. Alcohol is not something that makes them stumble in their relationship with God. However, if someone *does* struggle with drinking too much and this is a habitual pattern, it might be wise for them to avoid going to bars or having a drink with their dinner.

This is not an issue that is black and white. It must be assessed on an individual basis. We have to be honest with ourselves and our church family about what our limitations are and where we need help so as to not fall into patterns of habitual sin. Sometimes it is not that we have to literally remove something from our life. Sometimes it is that we have to remove it from having such a strong influence over us. For example, maybe we are close to someone who influences our life in very negative and destructive ways. In some cases we may have to cut that person completely out of our life. In some cases we may just have to spend less time with them or be more careful about the type of settings in which we spend time with that person. There are all kinds of ways we can remove something from influencing us in ways that it shouldn't.

James tells us not only to put away all filthiness, he also tells us to put away all "superfluity of naughtiness." The reason we sin is not primarily because of the things we surround ourselves with. We sin because of what is in our heart. While it is true we must be careful about what we surround ourselves with, changing what we surround ourselves with and changing our behavior cannot bring the change we need to have happen. Our real problem is our desire. Outside influences serve to spark desires in our heart, but the explosion caused by that spark is due to the volatile substance within our hearts known as sin. This internal sin has roots that go deep in our heart. Our thoughts and beliefs are, at the deepest level, our life's base. Because we are born as sinners, these thoughts and beliefs continue to saturate our life until they are uprooted and replaced with the truth. We are born in ignorance and remain there until the truth invades and saturates deep into our heart.

This is exactly why James exhorts us to do the third thing, which is to "receive with meekness the engrafted word." The best way to rid ourselves of the evil that tempts us and dwells within us is by filling ourselves with the truth. God opened our eyes and brought us to life through the gospel. The Holy Spirit caused "the engrafted word" to take root in our heart. And when the gospel took hold of us, who we were, down to our very roots, changed. We became a new person. The way change happens—real, lasting change—is the same way we are saved: through the gospel.

The gospel is not something we receive once and then are good-to-go for the rest of our life. The gospel is something we have to receive over and over. It has to soak into every layer of our heart. Our sin is like the layers of an onion. Once the gospel peels away one layer of the sin that covers our heart, there is another layer underneath it that needs to have the gospel peel it away. We need to hear the gospel consistently—every day—or it will not have much effect on our daily life.

The act of turning away from our sin and receiving the gospel go together hand-in-hand. They go together like a hand in a glove; they are a perfect fit; they were made to go together. The gospel is what saves us, and the gospel is what changes us. Through God's grace we work out our salvation, laboring with his strength at work inside us. We are not fighting *for* victory, we are fighting *from* victory. The victory has already been won. Let's persevere in our faith, knowing that we already have the victory over our sin.

Scripture has a Purpose
(James 1:22-25)

Additional Reading: 2 Corinthians 3:8; 2 Timothy 3:16-17; Deuteronomy 29:29

It was a dream come true. A brand new car was just dropped off in his driveway. Jeremy could not believe it. It was a free gift from someone. The taxes and all costs had been paid. The car was free—absolutely free. It was the car he had dreamed about for the past year. And now it was his. Jeremy marveled at the car sitting in his driveway. He spent hours upon hours walking around the car looking at it and touching it. Yet Jeremy rarely drove it. It was the only car he had, yet he chose to not use it. Not having a car was a huge inconvenience. It made his life very difficult. He couldn't get to work or go to the grocery store without having to go through a long and difficult process to get where he wanted to go. His friend gave him the car so he could drive it, but he was content to just walk around the car and admire it.

What is wrong with this scenario? What was Jeremy's problem? What is wrong with this scenario is that Jeremy did not use the car for the purpose for which it was given. He was given a wonderful gift, yet he did not reap the gift's benefits. He did not use the car in a way that truly helped him.

It can often be easy to use Scripture in the same way Jeremy used his car: we are not using it for the purpose for which it is given to us. We want Scripture to entertain us, to make us feel good, and to tell us interesting things—but we often fall into the trap of neglecting the real reason God gave us Scripture. Scripture was given to us to teach us about

54

life and how to live. Everything in Scripture serves that purpose. Through revealing Christ to us (which is the primary purpose of Scripture), we are shown who God is and how we are supposed to relate to him.

Scripture serves as a mirror. It reveals a lot of things. One way Scripture is a mirror is its revelation of who we were made to be and how we were made to live. Humans are made in the Image of God. This means everything humans do is done in relation to God. We were made to reflect God's glory and to represent him by having dominion over the earth. We were made to demonstrate his moral character through our words and actions. We have been made to rule and reign over the earth. Everything on earth was intended to be under the subjection of human beings. We were made to engage in our day-to-day activities in such a way that God's glory would spread throughout the entire earth. Our activities and creative endeavors were meant to display how awesome, good and beautiful God is.

Through Scripture revealing how we are supposed to live, it reveals something else about us: we do not live the way God intended for us to. We fall short of his standards. Humans have been made in the Image of God. This means that we were made to answer God when he is speaking. Scripture and our conscience reveal what God is speaking. In doing so it also reveals that even though God is speaking, we have not been responding to him. We were made in a loving, covenant relationship with God. A covenant is a legal, oath-based agreement. A covenant is a legal relationship that has stipulations. Humans were made to know God and glorify him. Yet all of us have broken God's covenant.

Scripture reveals who we were made to be, how we are meant to live and how short we fall of God's standards. Scripture also reveals something else. Scripture reveals our Savior Jesus Christ. Jesus delivers us from the penalty of our sin and restores our covenant relationship with God. Through seeing the great love that God has shown us in Jesus, we are transformed more and more into the person God created us to be. We become doers of the law who freely obey God from our heart. We become people who devote ourselves to the one thing that can satisfy our soul: the glory of God.

Better than being a master of Scripture, is being mastered by the One who wrote it--the One who loves us enough to show us how he has made us to live, and the One who loves us enough to cover and pay for all the times we don't live how he intends. Open your Bible to behold the face of its Author. And then respond to his great love by putting what he says into action.

Free to Obey (James 1:25)

Additional Reading: John 8:34-35; Romans 6:12-20

When I was a child and a teenager, I had a lot of difficulty understanding some of the things my parents did. I had a lot of trouble understanding why they put certain expectations around my sister and me; expectations they put around us to protect us from harm and to lead us to maturity. My parents were incessant about my sister and me finishing what we had started. I remember one year I was on a basketball team and I desperately wanted to quit. The team was not doing well. I was tired of playing, and my frequent sicknesses that winter took a toll on me physically. Needless to say, I was ready for that basketball season to be over. My parents would not let me quit. They told me that if I had committed myself to do something, and it was within my ability to fulfill that commitment, then I needed to do what I said I would do. My parents also were very intolerant of lying. They were very adamant about my sister and me being honest and truthful in what we said and did. They really strived to drive home the point that it is very difficult to trust someone who is not honest or truthful with their words. They showed my sister and me that it is best to tell the truth because the lies we tell will eventually be exposed; that lying would really only make life more difficult for us in the long run.

My parents were not, and are not, perfect people. But there are a lot of things they did as parents that I will likely do if I ever have children of my own. And there are some things that I will likely not do if I ever have children of my own. My parents had some successes and some shortcomings. All parents do. But one of the things my parents did very well was driving home the fact that freedom comes through obedience. My parents really helped me see that rules and laws are supposed to be things that were put in place for my good. They helped me realize that rather than rules and laws restricting my freedom, they actually are the very things that can lead me to freedom—true freedom.

James is telling us this very same thing my parents taught me. James calls God's law "the perfect law of liberty." While the law can do nothing to make us right with God or earn us his favor, there is a sense in which obeying the law is freedom. When we have been born again, we have the ability to obey God from our heart. Being able to love, serve and obey God is freedom because that is what we were created to do.

Too often we read an American idea of freedom into Scripture. We believe that freedom is the ability to do whatever we want. We believe that freedom consists in having the right to life, liberty and the pursuit of happiness. But Scripture defines freedom in a much different way. Freedom is fundamentally not the ability to do what we want. We are guided and controlled by our desires. We choose what we choose by necessity because our choices are merely the fruit of our nature. Our nature is the root. Our choices are the fruit of that root.

Scripture defines freedom as being free from the power and tyranny of sin. The only person who is free is he who is a slave of righteousness. The only person who is free is he whose heart is captivated by Jesus. We are only free—truly free—when we love and obey God, which is what we were created to do.

Rejoice not that you have the freedom to choose what you desire. For if God had not intervened in our life by softening our heart and opening up our eyes to the truth and beauty of the gospel, the only thing any of us would freely choose would be sin. And the end result of that would be destruction. Apart from miraculous, divine intervention we would have freely continued on our crash course to hell—and that is the only thing we would have chosen to do. Boasting about having free will is foolish. Yes, we have the ability to do what we want to do. But God does not call being free to do what we want, freedom. Sin is slavery. Being free to choose sin is slavery. The type of freedom that Scripture presents to us is freedom from sin. Scripture says everything other than being free to love and obey God is bondage. It is not freedom.

Rejoice that the grace of God shattered the blinders that were over the eyes of your heart. Rejoice that God gave you a heart that desires him. Rejoice that you have been given a heart that desires God and knows that it was made for God. Rejoice that you are free—truly free—to pursue the one and only thing that can satisfy your soul: God.

Made for God (James 1:25)

Additional Reading: 1 John 4:7-9; Romans 13:8-10;
Matthew 22:34-40; Jeremiah 31:33

There are times in life when what *feels* loving is unloving, and what does not *feel* loving actually *is* loving. I remember when I was growing up, I would sometimes envy some of my friends because of the freedom their parents gave them. I envied the warmth with which their parents would say, "Sure. Go ahead. Do what you want." In my naïveté, I assumed they were better parents than mine. I assumed my parents just weren't hip and "with it." I thought they were out of the loop. I had no doubt that they loved me; it just seemed to me they were living under a rock and did not understand the world I was living in. There were things they did not allow me to do. There were places they would not allow me to hang out. There were clothes they would not allow me to wear. There were movies they did not want me to watch. There was music they did not want me to listen to.

Through and through I knew that what motivated my parents to do the things they did was love. I knew they loved me, cared about me and wanted good things for me. And while at the time I did not understand some of the things they did, now that I am older I very clearly see why they did it. Every now and then I run into some of these friends or their parents. And when I do, my parents' reasons for raising me the way they did is crystal clear. While my friends' parents treated them in ways that seemed loving, what they were doing was unloving and very unhealthy. When I see these friends whom I so dearly loved now in jail, burnt out on drugs or having wrecked their life by their bad decisions, my heart breaks for them. And I praise God that by his grace I am not where they are today. I am not perfect and I have not always made wise choices, but God spared me from a lot of trouble and heartache because of how my parents raised me.

I remember one time when I had just become old enough to stay home by myself. I told my mom I did not want to go to church that Sunday. My parents talked this over amongst themselves and told me that they were not going to force me to go to church if I did not want to go. They did not tell me how disappointed they were or how I should want to go to church. They did not try to give me a guilt trip either. I ended up going to church that Sunday. Why? Because I knew it was important to my parents. I did not understand why going to church was important to them, but I knew they loved me and wanted what was best for me. I saw that choosing not to go to church made them very sad. I knew that they loved and accepted me just as I am. I knew that if what I was doing was causing them hurt then maybe they had good reasons for wanting me to make different choices.

Sometimes what God asks of us does not seem very loving. Sometimes it seems more like a burden and a nuisance than it seems like love. Sometimes we don't understand why God has given us the boundaries he has put around us. Sometimes we think God is unhip and should catch up with the times. But God knows better than we do. He sees a much bigger picture than we do. He is wiser than we are. He loves us more deeply than we could ever imagine. And the things he commands us to do are motivated by his deep love for us.

James calls God's law "the perfect law of liberty." Why does James refer to God's law in this way? James refers to the law this way because the law reveals God's character to us. God is love. His law reveals to us how we can live a life that loves him and the people he has put in our life. The heart of his law is love. The way we obey God's law is by living a life of love.

The law is the "perfect law" because our relationship with God is not based on whether or not we keep his law. Our relationship with God is based on Christ having met the requirements of the law on our behalf. God's law is perfect because it reveals his character and how he intends for us to live. The law is the "law of liberty" because we can obey God out of love and gratitude rather than out of compulsion. Hymn writer William Cowper talks about this very beautifully in his hymn "Love Constrained to Obedience":

> *"To see the law by Christ fulfilled,*
> *To hear His pardoning voice,*
> *Changes a slave into a child,*
> *And duty into choice."*

When we became born again, we received a new nature. We became spiritually alive. We became a new person at the very core of who we are. We received a nature that is sensitive to the things of God. We began to have new desires. We began to not like the things we used to do before we were saved. For the first time in our life we became truly able to obey God. For the first time in our life we became able to truly love other people. This became possible for us because God put in us a new nature that delights in knowing him and making him known.

Often the reason we are restless and discontent in life is due to us trying to live for our own kingdom. Living for our own kingdom goes against the new nature that God has put inside us. We were made to live a life of love. Through Jesus we are able to love as God intended. Because Jesus fulfilled "the perfect law" on our behalf, we are at liberty to obey God and live a life of love. God has given us his law to show us what love looks like; to guide and direct our lives. He has also given us his law to show us our need for a savior. We don't live a life of love a lot of the time, which is proof that we need a savior. God not only provides us with his law to direct our life, he also sent Jesus to fulfill the requirements of that law on our behalf. And because of his great love for us we can respond to him by obeying his law out of love and gratitude. What we once considered to merely be our duty becomes our delight. God's love and fatherly kindness changes us from the inside out. Look to Jesus and respond to his love by obeying him out of the gratitude you have for what he has done for you.

The Blessing of Obedience
(James 1:25)

Additional Reading: Psalm 34:11-14; Luke 11:27-28; Galatians 6:7-9

Every summer while I was growing up my family grew a huge garden. Summer was a time we all looked forward to because we got to eat a lot of fresh vegetables that came from our garden. There is nothing quite like fresh tomatoes and squash from your very own garden. Every spring we had to till the soil so the ground would be in a condition that would allow plants to grow. Once the ground was tilled and the weeds had been rooted out, we had to draw up a plan to determine what we were going to plant and where we were going to plant it in the garden. Each crop was put in its own section.

The funny thing about seeds is that whatever kind of seed you put into the ground will be the kind of plant you get. If you plant squash seeds into the ground what will grow is a plant that produces squash. And if you plant the seeds that are produced from that plant, the result will be more plants that produce squash. If you keep planting the seeds each plant produces, you will have a never-ending supply of squash. Your squash supply will never end, and it will continue to keep growing larger and larger.

A garden is a great analogy for how our spiritual life works. We are saved entirely by grace. At the same time, God set up the universe to operate on the principle of justice; God set up the universe to operate on the principle of sowing and reaping. Whatever we sow into our lives is what we will reap.

It is a lot like karma: we get out of life what we put into it. Not only will we reap what we sow, what we sow will multiply. Sowing seeds always results in a harvest. Always. If we sow bitterness and unforgiveness into our relationships, we will reap relationships that lack intimacy.

If we sow into our life things that seek to satisfy our sinful desires, we will reap a harvest of even more sinful desires. Feeding sinful desires is a lot like feeding my friend's fat Chihuahua. I have a friend who has the fattest dog I have ever seen. His Chihuahua does not know when to stop eating. The dog will eat until he makes himself absolutely sick. And after he makes himself sick by eating too much, he eats some more. The more he eats, the bigger his stomach gets. The bigger his stomach gets the more he eats, which has only led to him eating more and more. Nothing is able to satisfy that Chihuahua's appetite. Our sinful desires are like my friend's Chihuahua: feeding his appetite inevitably only leads to his appetite getting bigger. Sin produces in us more and more sin.

The converse of this is also true. Our obedience to God leads to more obedience. Obedience aligns us with how God designed us to live. Obedience allows the scales of justice that undergird the fabric of the universe to begin to tip in our favor. It is not that we earn God's favor or that our obedience has any inherent worth that somehow adds to God's love and acceptance of us. Even our best obedience is stained with sin and must be cleansed by the blood of Jesus. Rather, when we obey God we tap into the fundamental reality of how this world was designed to operate. It works much like ships making use of natural, powerful currents to get them where they want to go. If they follow the direction of the current, it is easier for them to get to the place they intend. Sin is a lot like the Bermuda Triangle. If you get sucked into it, you may never be heard from again. The storms of life will overtake you and make a shipwreck of your life. But if you have a powerful current giving you a boost in the direction you want to go, it is more likely you will reach your destination safely.

Obeying God often works to our advantage. Think about this from a logical perspective. There are two people who work for you whom you are considering giving a promotion. The promotion involves giving that person a lot of responsibility and freedom over a very large amount of money. Person #1 is very smart, but he does as little work as he can get away with. He has more experience than Person #2, but he is lazy. Also, his integrity is questionable, as he has a track record for being dishonest when it is to his advantage. Person #2 does not have all of the experience that Person #1 has. But Person #2 is a hard worker. She is diligent. She is humble and wise enough to know when to ask for help if she thinks she might need it. Person #2 has always shown integrity in her interactions and has apologized for the wrongs she has done. She is honest even when being honest is to her disadvantage.

To which candidate would you give the promotion? Person #2 makes the better candidate. She can gain experience. Person #1 might swindle your company out of a lot of money and end up doing irreparable damage to your company. Sometimes people like Person #1 do get the promotion. But eventually they will reap what they have sown. In the long run, only Person #2 will have any lasting success. Being like Person #1 will only do us harm in the end. Disobedient people who seem to be the most successful are usually the most miserable people, and are also usually the most miserable people to be around.

Why would we ever want to be a slave of sin and idolatry when we can live in the freedom we were always meant to have? True joy comes from knowing God and making him known. Even if no material benefit ever came to us because of our obedience, living out our faith in obedience to God would be well worth it. We would never come to the end of our life regretting having lived our life for something that will outlive our life. The pursuit of personal gain is short-sighted. Everyone who lives their life for their own interests will one day see clearly that they have wasted their life. No one has ever said on their deathbed that they wish they'd spent more time at work or that they wish they'd had the opportunity to have a nicer car before they died.

Obeying God makes our life impact where the ripples from it will be felt for all eternity. Being a doer of the word aligns us with God's purpose for our life: to glorify and enjoy God. Even when obeying God is costly, it is by no means as costly as disobedience is. The harvest of destruction that we will reap from our disobedience is not worth the short-lived pleasure we might temporarily gain. True joy, freedom and prosperity are found through obeying God. Our obedience is meant to lead us into a place where we glorify God and enjoy him more and more. Be a doer of the word. You will be blessed by it.

The Mouth is the Way to the Heart (James 1:26)

Additional Reading: Matthew 6:1; Luke 6:43-45

Several years ago as I drove down the highway one day my Check Engine light came on. So I pulled over to see what was wrong with my car. I lifted the hood of my car, checked over everything to see if it was okay, and then I closed my hood and got back into my car. I turned the key and the Check Engine light was no longer on.

In the weeks that followed, this same thing kept happening over and over. So I took the car to the shop to see if a mechanic could find the problem. The mechanic searched and searched for the problem but did not find anything wrong with my car. He eventually discovered the problem was a defective sensor making my Check Engine light come on. My engine was fine. I just had a bad sensor giving me false information.

It was going to cost around 300 dollars to fix the faulty sensor. I figured I would save my money by not replacing the sensor. Besides, I knew of a redneck service station that would be willing to let my car pass the State Inspection with a bad sensor. Letting a car that has a bad sensor pass the State Inspection is technically illegal, but in a county that lets kids drive their tractors and lawnmowers to school something like a bad sensor would not have caused too much of a stir. While a bad sensor can be ignored, there is one thing a bad sensor cannot do: tell you when there actually is a problem. After being stranded on the side of the road a few times, I decided that paying the 300 dollars to fix the sensor maybe was not such a huge inconvenience after all.

The human heart is a lot like the faulty sensor in my car. Even with the Holy Spirit guiding us and convicting us of our sin, there are two characteristics above all others that describe the human heart: "deceitful above all things, and desperately wicked" (Jeremiah 17:9). We not only fool other people about who we really are, we also fool ourselves. Our heart sensor often does not give an accurate reading of what is really going on inside of us.

The reason this is so dangerous is that it blinds us of the true condition of our heart. We can believe that just because we are doing the right things our heart is okay. We can be "doers of the word" in a way where we are actually serving ourselves rather than God. We can be doing the right things for the wrong reasons—and not even be aware we are doing that. So how do we get an accurate reading of where our heart is spiritually?

A good test of where we are spiritually is what comes out of our mouth. What we say flows out of what is in our heart. If you want to get a good feel for where you are spiritually, listen to what you say.

How do you respond when you are inconvenienced by another person?

How do you respond when someone sins against you or offends you?

Does what you say communicate grace to the people you are speaking to?

When do you find yourself wanting to lie? What do you lie about?

Does what you communicate draw attention to yourself or to God? Is what you are saying aiming to build up your kingdom or God's kingdom?

Are your words pure? Are your words building people up or are they bent towards criticism?

We are saved entirely by grace. What James is talking about in this verse is how we know we are doing the right things with the right motives. All true obedience is the result of God's grace having changed our heart. James is aiming this statement at people who play religious games by pretending they are a better person than they actually are. James is aiming this verse at people who are not concerned about their heart. James is saying, "If you think you are doing the right things but your mouth is full of words that are bitter, hateful, critical, demeaning or disgusting, then your obedience is not real because your mouth reveals you are not doing the right things with the right motives. Your mouth is exposing what is really in your heart."

James is NOT saying that if we slip-up and say things we shouldn't, then we are not saved. James is saying that our words will expose our actions if our actions are being done out of wrong motives. The more God's love soaks into our heart the more our words and actions begin to change. The process of our words and actions genuinely changing is usually a very slow and difficult process. Change happens over time as a response to the love and acceptance God has already given us. This is how the Christian life is designed to be. If what you say troubles you, James is likely not talking about you in this verse. The fact that you are troubled is a good thing. It shows that God is at work within you. Run to Christ and ask him to cleanse your heart and help you change.

Our mouth is our motive monitor. If your mouth is revealing to you that some of your motives for doing the right things are wrong, then ask God to search your heart and show you what your motivations actually are. Ask God to forgive you for doing the right things with the wrong motivation. Ask God to help you to do the right things out of love and gratitude for who he is and what he has done for you. Ask him to help you stop pretending and start being more honest about who you really are.

Everyone has some inconsistency between what they say and what they do. This will always be the case for our entire life. Expect it. But also know that your mouth is a tool you can use to help yourself grow. Pay attention to your words. When your heart is revealed through what you say and the picture is not pretty, examine your heart and turn to Christ so he can cleanse your heart and help you change. Even when we are saying things we should not be saying, our mouth is still a tool that helps lead us to see our need for God. Our mouth can be a tool that leads us back to God, both by revealing our heart to us and by confessing to God our need for him. Even when our words expose the ugly things that are in our heart we can praise him for giving us a tool that points us back to our need for him.

True Religion (James 1:27)

Additional Reading: 1 John 2:15-17; Psalm 68:5-6;
Hebrews 12:14

What is the essence of what God wants our life
to look like? God wants us to be his representatives
on this earth. He wants our life to display who he is.
Two ways we display what God is like are through our
actions and through our character. Our action,
character and love can set us apart in such a way that
the world notices God's beauty being reflected
through us.

First, God desires us to "visit the fatherless and
widows in their affliction." What does this mean?
Quite literally, it means we are to take care of widows
and the fatherless. Why is this so important? In
James' time widows and the fatherless were society's
most helpless and defenseless people. These were
also the people who often needed someone to be
their advocate; they needed someone to stand up and
defend them. There are a lot of things they are not
able to do themselves. I remember once, when
working one-on-one with people who have
developmental disabilities, my client's parents were
illiterate; their reading and writing skills were minimal.
It was very difficult for them to access the various
government resources available to help support their
child's specific needs. I often had to help navigate
these resources so their child could be helped. This
often involved me acting on their behalf in their best
interest.

God desires us to help the weak and
defenseless because he helped us when we were

weak and defenseless. God sent Jesus into the world to break the power of sin which bound us. We were fatherless. God was not our Father. We had chosen to leave the family of God. Sin had broken our relationship with God. We were without a husband. We broke our covenant with God by whoring around with other gods. We gave ourselves away to things other than God. We spread the legs of our souls and packed up our stuff to go make our home with lovers less wild than God. We had forsaken the Creator to shack-up with the things he had created. God was as good as dead to us. There was a Great Divorce that split through the cosmos, separating us from God.[1] God was no longer our husband. He was no longer our protector. He was no longer our provider. We were cast out; helpless, hopeless and defenseless against the power of sin and the devil. But God sent Jesus into the world so we could be adopted back into his family. God sent Jesus so we could be his bride; a bride that is waiting on Jesus, our bridegroom, to return. Jesus defended us when we were defenseless. Jesus helped us when we were helpless. Jesus gave us hope when we were in a hopeless situation. Jesus became our advocate when nothing stood between us and the fury of our Almighty God's wrath.

When we help widows and the fatherless we are living out and putting on display what the heart of the gospel looks like. We are giving the world a picture of what God desires to do in our lives spiritually. God helps those who cannot help themselves. He calls us to do the same thing. God wants us to be involved in the world; to show mercy to those in need of mercy. In this verse James mentions helping widows and the fatherless, but by saying this he means to communicate to us that the essence of true religion is contained in loving and serving others with the same kind of love Christ has shown us.

While God wants us to be involved in serving the messy, broken world around us, we are also not to do this in a way that causes us to compromise who we are. We become stained by the world when we let the world's mindset soak into our hearts and saturate into who we are and how we live. We are to be distinct from the world. We are to be directly involved in the world while being different in who we are, how we live and how we respond to the situations we encounter.

When the world hates, we will love with the same love Christ has for us. When the world stirs up strife, we will extend peace and seek to reconcile others with the same type of reconciliation God extends to us in Christ. When the world grows frustrated and impatient, we will display the same patience that God shows to us and our shortcomings. When the world is cruel and unkind, we will be kind with the same type of kindness God gives us to lead us to repentance. When the world exploits others and is out for their own interests, we will show the goodness of God by looking out for the interests of others; by blessing other people and by living a life that shows the wholeness God has given to our heart. In a world where promises are often broken and obligations often are not fulfilled in the way they should be, we will be people who show the faithfulness of God through our words and actions. We will do what we say we will do and fulfill our obligations to the best of our ability. In a world that is harsh and reckless, we will be people who deal with the weaknesses of others with the same gentleness

74

that God shows us. In a world where people are controlled by their desires, we will show the world the freedom Christ gives us by exercising self-control. Instead of the things God created ruling over us, we will rule over them. This is how God designed us to live.

Instead of being conformed to this world, we will live a life that has been transformed by the power of God. Our life will be so different that people will see God in us. Through our actions and character, people will catch glimpses of what God is really like. The world will see us as a light that pierces through the darkness. The world will see us as a light that is pointing them to their true home and true Father.

Prejudiced (James 2:1-13)

Additional Reading: 2 Corinthians 5:14-17; Exodus 20:1-17

One of the things I learned in college is that I am prejudiced. No, I am not racist or sexist. And my college education did not open me up to adopting a liberal worldview where I became accepting of all lifestyles. Although that was the goal of many of my professors, they were not successful. Nevertheless, I learned that I truly am prejudiced.

I went to college to study social work. Social work is a field in which you must interact with people from all walks of life. In several of my classes we often discussed the need to be aware of our own biases and prejudices so we could be aware of the things that are influencing the decisions we make. Social workers are forced to make a lot of difficult, ethical decisions that usually do not have any clear, easy solutions. And these decisions social workers must make affect other people's lives. Needless to say, a social worker needs to be aware of why they are making these decisions; the reasons must be legitimate ones.

In several of my classes we did exercises that, sometimes rather painfully, revealed the prejudices and biases we had. One of the things that really stood out to my classmates and me after these exercises was the reality that everyone has prejudices and biases. People who say they do not have prejudices are usually prejudiced against those who show that trait openly. Having prejudices and biases is a normal part of life. It is a reality of the condition of our heart.

That's not to say it is right to have prejudices. It is just that we are fooling ourselves if we think we do

76

not have any. Part of learning to not act upon our prejudices is being aware that we do have them. Being aware of our prejudices and biases helps give us clarity to notice when we are being tempted to show favoritism.

Favoritism was a problem in the churches James led. During his time, society was dominated by social castes and wealthy landowners. The people at the top of the food chain in society were wealthy. It was much like it is today, only more pronounced and with much less possibility of advancing to a higher social class.

A lot of the people in the churches James led suffered persecution and hardship. Because of their devotion to Christ they were cut off from all ties to their family, work, temple and synagogue; Jewish Christians experienced their families, friends and religious community turn their backs on them. All of Jewish life was centered upon family ties and religion. These two aspects went hand in hand and bled into every aspect of the life of a Jewish person. Forsaking Judaism was a dream-wrecker. Forsaking Judaism would cut a person off from every relationship and connection in life, and it could happen in an instant. These Jewish Christians had little-to-no support other than that their church provided.

Despite the difficulties some of these Jewish Christians were facing, people within the church began to show favoritism toward those who were wealthy. They were treating the poor believers in their church family like second-class citizens. The wealthy people in their midst got treated very well while the poor people were being overlooked and treated unfairly. The poor believers were being judged because of their outward appearance. They were looked down upon because they did not have the nicest clothes. Their social standing in the world influenced how they were treated in the church.

How often we do the same type of thing! We treat our fellow believers better if they agree with us about worship style. If they will not worship God the same way that we do, we separate from them. We divide the church by starting a new service that will suit our tastes. We go to churches that create environments that inevitably create generational and cultural gaps. It is often said that Sunday morning is the most segregated time of the week. We choose people to lead the church whose qualifications are based more upon their position in the world rather than upon the evidence of God having changed their life. We turn our noses up at people who disagree with us about doctrines that are not truly essential to our faith. We look on disdain at those who do not come to church dressed with the clothes we think are stylish. Younger people assume that the older people in the church are simply "out of touch." Older people assume they know what life is like for younger people. They are not willing to look at the complexities that have been added to life since the time they were in their prime.

People within the church in James' generation placed value on the things the world valued. They compromised with the world. They sought acceptance from the world in a way that compromised the truth that everyone who is in Christ is equal, regardless of their ethnicity, gender, looks or economic status. They disregarded parts of God's law in order to justify treating the poor believers unfairly. Whether they were openly disregarding parts of God's law or whether they were just overlooking their sin is irrelevant. At the heart of the matter, their problem was they were attempting to be the judge and jury to decide for themselves what was right and wrong. They wanted to have the final say over how people should be treated.

The problem with making up the rules ourselves is that disregarding parts of God's law is the same thing as disregarding the God who gave us the law. God's law is a reflection of who he is; God's law reveals his character. When we try to justify our actions by overlooking certain parts of God's law, we are rejecting God himself. We cannot divorce God's law from God.

Trying to excuse ourselves by classifying sins misses the whole point of obeying God in the first place. God is not pleased by us avoiding the "big" sins but then throwing mud in his face by living our life committing "little" sins. We cannot tip the cosmic scales of justice in our favor by avoiding certain sins. The reason we seek to obey God is out of gratitude for what he has done. We are guilty before God because his law demands from us perfect obedience. We have all failed to obey God in one way or another. We are all guilty in God's courtroom.

Even though we are all guilty, God still accepts us and welcomes us into his family. He accepts and welcomes us into his family because he is good. He accepts us and welcomes us into his family because Jesus has perfectly obeyed the law on our behalf and took on the punishment we deserve. He accepts us and welcomes us into his family irrespective of anything about us. He accepts us and welcomes us into his family in spite of the way we have turned our backs on him. And he accepts us and welcomes us into his family even though we still turn our backs on him from time to time; even now.

God's law is a law of love. That is its very essence. And even when we rejected God's wise and loving directions for our life, God showed us just how amazing his love is by having mercy on us. He did not treat us how we deserve to be treated. He himself bore the cost of reconciling us to himself by sending Jesus. There are no requirements we must meet in order to be accepted into his family.

Therefore he is impartial toward all people. He extends to each of us the same invitation of new life. He does not put us off until we measure-up to his standards. No, he gladly accepts us just as we are. He himself broke down every barrier that separated us from him. It is all of grace.

This is the type of love that demands a response from us. As an old hymn puts it,

> "Were the whole realm of nature mine,
> That were a present far too small;
> Love so amazing, so divine,
> Demands my soul, my life, my all."[2]

The love that God has shown us through Jesus strips us of having any reason to show partiality toward people based on external things like economic or social status, ethnicity, gender, clothing or appearance.

Jesus' death on the cross frees us from the legal demands of the law so that our obedience is something we can now offer freely from a heart transformed by God's grace. When we see the expectations God has for humanity and how abundantly he met those expectations in Jesus' life and death, any expectations we put on other people are seen for what they are: frivolous and petty. We have mercy on one another by not showing partiality. The wideness of the love and mercy God has shown to us so freely is the only thing that can free us to have love and mercy for other people; a love that is wide enough to treat all people in our church and life with impartiality.

Do not turn a blind eye to the fact that you have prejudices and biases. Do not pretend that they do not exist. Prejudices and biases run deep within the human heart. Acknowledge that you have them. Bring them out into light. Where prejudices and biases have been borne in your heart because of past hurts, bring those wounds to Jesus. He can bring healing and freedom to your hurting heart. Where prejudices and biases are in your heart because of your own selfishness, confess those sins to God. He promises to forgive and cleanse us from the sin we confess to him. Pour the weight of the gospel over that sin. Let the weight of God's grace crush those idols until they become dust beneath your feet. Let the freedom Christ has given to you overtake you like a mighty rushing river that washes away your biases and prejudices. Let the love of God come into the deepest parts of your heart so that you become freer and freer to truly love people with the love God has always intended for us to have for one another. Don't turn away. Turn to Christ. Turn to freedom.

Are All Sins Equal? (James 2:10-11)

One of the main rules for interpreting a passage of Scripture is to look at the passage in light of what the rest of Scripture says. Scripture will never truly contradict Scripture. If we interpret a passage of Scripture in a way that contradicts what the rest of Scripture says, then our interpretation is wrong.

At face value, James 2:10-11 seems to be saying that all sins are equal. Are all sins equal in God's eyes? Yes, and no. All sins are equal in the sense that they all make us guilty before God. For example, if you have driven over the speed limit or have murdered someone, in both instances you have broken the law. You would be guilty of breaking the law. In both instances you deserve to receive the consequences for your actions. Breaking the speed limit does not deserve the same punishment that murder deserves, but both crimes will make you guilty in a court of law. The only way to have no consequence is to not break any law whatsoever. God requires perfect obedience. Scripture tells us that the wages of sin is death. So any sin will condemn us and separate us from God's blessing. In terms of legal guilt, all sins are equally bad in that they separate us from God's blessing and condemn us.

With that said, some sins are worse than others. God hates all sin, but he does not hate all sin equally. All sin makes us guilty before God, but not all sin deserves the same punishment. There are a variety of reasons God does not render the same punishment for every sin. Because God is a God of justice, he cannot punish every sin as though they are all equally bad.

Some sins are worse than others because of the knowledge we have when we commit them. God will not hold us responsible for something we have no knowledge of. The more God has revealed to us, the more responsibility we have to do something with what he has shown us. For example, Judas Iscariot was one of Jesus' closest disciples. Judas Iscariot was with Jesus every day for a few years. Judas saw the miracles that Jesus did. Judas had every reason to believe that Jesus was the Messiah. Judas heard Jesus teach about the nature of the Kingdom of God. Judas should have understood that Jesus did not come to set up an earthly Kingdom at that point in time. Pontius Pilate was the ruler who allowed Jesus to be delivered over to be crucified. Pilate did not spend any time with Jesus. Pilate likely did not hear Jesus teach about the nature of God's Kingdom. Pilate might not have ever heard Jesus teach at all. Jesus' response to a question Pilate asked him is very revealing.

> **"Jesus answered, Thou couldest have no power at all against me, except it were given thee from above: therefore he that delivered me unto thee hath the greater sin."** John 19:11

Judas knew more about Jesus than Pilate did. Therefore, Judas' sin was worse than Pilate's. Jesus said things similar to this earlier in his ministry.

> **"Then began he to upbraid the cities wherein most of his mighty works were done, because they repented not:**

Woe unto thee, Chorazin! woe unto thee, Bethsaida! for if the mighty works, which were done in you, had been done in Tyre and Sidon, they would have repented long ago in sackcloth and ashes. But I say unto you, It shall be more tolerable for Tyre and Sidon at the day of judgment, than for you. And thou, Capernaum, which art exalted unto heaven, shalt be brought down to hell: for if the mighty works, which have been done in thee, had been done in Sodom, it would have remained until this day. But I say unto you, That it shall be more tolerable for the land of Sodom in the day of judgment, than for thee." Matthew 11:20-24

"And that servant, which knew his lord's will, and prepared not himself, neither did according to his will, shall be beaten with many stripes. But he that knew not, and did commit things worthy of stripes, shall be beaten with few stripes. For unto whomsoever much is given, of him shall be much required: and to whom men have committed much, of him they will ask the more." Luke 12:47-48

Hebrews 10:28-29 explains that people who know of the revelation of God's offer of forgiveness through Christ, but then reject that forgiveness, will deserve a worse punishment than those who only had the revelation of God's forgiveness offered through the Old Testament sacrificial law.

"He that despised Moses' law died without mercy under two or three witnesses: Of how much sorer punishment, suppose ye, shall he be thought worthy, who hath trodden under foot the Son of God, and hath counted the blood of the covenant, wherewith he was sanctified, an unholy thing, and hath done despite unto the Spirit of grace?" Hebrews 10:28-29

A greater revelation of God's forgiveness warrants a greater response. A rejection of this great revelation warrants a greater punishment than the punishment that was previously prescribed.

While it is true that some sins are worse than others, Scripture does not list which sins are the worst. Listing sins and trying to avoid the worst ones misses the point of why God gave us the law or the gospel. This is probably why God did not give us a list.

Generally speaking, the sins that bring God the most displeasure are the ones that bring the most harm to people. Human beings were made in God's Image. This means we were made to reflect who God is. We were made to reflect God's character through our character and the creative activities in which we engage, such as art or work. Sins against another person—especially against another person's humanity—are especially heinous because these sins are directly against the God in whose image people are created. Mark 12:38-40 alludes to condemnation being worse for people who intentionally prey upon the weak and helpless.

"And he said unto them in his doctrine, Beware of the scribes, which love to go in long clothing, and love salutations in the marketplaces, And the chief seats in the synagogues, and the uppermost rooms at feasts: Which devour widows' houses, and for a pretence make long prayers: these shall receive greater damnation." Mark 12:38-40

All sin condemns. All sin separates us from God's blessing. All sins are not equal, but all sin condemns us and hurts both us and the people around us. And all sin can be forgiven. All sin—no matter how bad it is—can be forgiven through receiving the forgiveness that God offers to us in Jesus Christ.

Are All Sins Equal? Part 2
(James 2:10-11)

Not all sins are equal in the sight of God. So what? What relevance does this have for our life? How does knowing this benefit us in any way? Knowing that all sins are not equal benefits us in a number of ways. It has a lot of practical value for the way we live.

One of the ways it benefits us is it helps us know the areas of our life where we need to put in the most effort to grow spiritually. Some sins have a more harmful effect on us and our relationships than other sins do. It is not that we should overlook any sin, but if we have to pick between putting in the effort either to obey the law of the land by not driving 10 miles over the speed limit or to be faithful to our spouse, it is more important that we focus most of our effort on being faithful to our spouse. Sins causing the most negative affect on us and our relationships should be the sins toward which we put the most effort to break free. It is not that we earn our freedom by striving to break free from our sin. Rather, it is that the most harmful sins in our life deserve the most personal attention. These are the sins we should seek God's help about the most. We should seek God about every area of our life. At the same time, we only have 24 hours every day. We have limited time and energy. We need to invest our time and energy seeking God on the issues that matter the most. God is more concerned about our relationship with our family than he is about the fact that we are addicted to caffeine. God would rather us spend time in prayer and in the Bible learning about how to best love our family than for us to spend that time praying and reading what the Bible has to say about our caffeine addiction. God wants to deal with both of those problems. But learning how to love our parents, spouse and children the way God wants us to is more important than our caffeine problem. God cares about us and our relationships. He does not want us to focus on the smaller issues in our life while the larger issues are destroying us and the people around us.

Another way this helps us is in realizing when to overlook a fault someone has and when to confront them. Sometimes the sin someone struggles with will be worked out the more that they grow in general. For example, someone might occasionally use their humor or knowledge to try to impress other people so that they will be accepted. Or someone might be prone to complain about people and circumstances difficult for them to deal with. These types of issues usually resolve themselves over time as the person continues to grow in their faith. If the fault is minor, it generally is wisest for us to overlook it. However, if the fault is having a destructive affect on the person themselves or the people around them, it might be best to prayerfully, gently and humbly find a way to confront them in private. Knowing when to overlook a fault in someone and when to confront them takes wisdom. It is not a black and white issue. Not every sin needs to be overlooked. And not every sin needs to be confronted. The Holy Spirit is able to convict people of their sin. Sometimes the Holy Spirit wants to use us to confront someone about their sin. Sometimes the Holy Spirit wants us to stay out of the way so that he can deal with the person in his own way and timing. Knowing that all sins are not equal frees us from feeling we have to confront or overlook every sin that is going on in someone's life.

There are several other reasons why it is beneficial for us to know why all sins are not equal, but we will deal with just one more reason. The concept of all sins not being equal provides the basis for the idea that "the punishment must fit the crime." What if every person who committed a crime received the same punishment regardless of the nature of the crime? What if people who committed cold-blooded murder and people who jaywalked both received the death penalty? What if the person who forgot to put on their seatbelt and the person who raped a ten-year-old child both only had to pay a fine? Would that be fair? Does a person who jaywalks deserve the death penalty? Should a child rapist only have to pay a fine for his crime? It seems absurd. Human governments know that the punishment must fit the crime. Justice demands that some crimes receive worse punishment than others. It is unjust to give the death penalty to someone who jaywalked. It is unjust to give a murderer the same punishment that someone should get for not wearing their seatbelt. To say that all sins are equal before God is to say that human governments are better at giving justice than God is.

To say that all sins are equal before God is also to say that human governments are more merciful than God is. God is more merciful to people who sin against him in ignorance than he is toward people who knowingly sin against him. In a court of law, if an adult who is severely mentally retarded comes up to a stranger and slaps them across the face, he will not be held accountable to the same degree as an adult who has a full mentality capacity.

Both people may know they are doing wrong, but there are circumstances surrounding the incident a judge would take into consideration. No judge in his right mind would send a severely mentally retarded person to jail for having slapped a stranger. The judge would show mercy to the person and offer alternative solutions that would help to prevent the incident from happening again. If biased, imperfect human judges in a court of law know that mercy must be shown because of the circumstances surrounding an incident, then surely God must treat us by the same standards.

God is a good Father who knows that the punishment must fit the crime. He desires those over whom we have authority be treated in this way. We must take into account the circumstances surrounding the misconduct of the person we have authority over. We must consider the nature and severity of the misbehavior. We must consider the knowledge the person who performed the act had at the time they did it. God wants us to imitate his justice in this regard. If God treats every sin the same, then on what basis can we distinguish how we are to respond to people who break God's law or the law of the land here on earth?

God is merciful, wise and just. God is reasonable. God is not an unjust judge who gives every offender the same punishment. Every person who breaks God's law and does not trust in Jesus will receive a life sentence to hell, but not every prisoner is treated the same. Just as prisoners in America do not all get the same treatment during their time of incarceration, so too God does not treat every unrepentant sinner the same way. Some prisoners are forced to do hard labor during their time behind bars while others are given jobs much less physically demanding. Some prisoners enjoy a level of freedom during their incarceration that other prisoners are never given. No sin will ever escape the justice of God, but no sin will escape the mercy of God either. All sin condemns us, but not all sins condemn us equally.

Not committing certain sins does not make us better than the people who do commit them. It is only by God's grace and mercy that we ourselves did not end up committing those same sins. We have no grounds to boast in this area whatsoever. Any good thing any of us has or does is solely because God's grace and mercy has restrained us and kept us from bringing ourselves to absolute ruin. All sin condemns. All sin does not condemn equally. But we must never forget that the only things keeping us from falling as far as other people have fallen are God's grace and mercy. Knowing this helps us to work for justice in ways that handle situations appropriately while also keeping us humble. It enables us to see clearly that we are just as prone to fall into the same type of sins as are other persons. We can acknowledge that some sins are more heinous than others, deal with situations appropriately and fairly, and treat the person humbly, extending to them the same grace and mercy we so desperately need.

There are many great benefits to knowing God doesn't view all sins equally. It takes a lot of wisdom to know how to best deal with the sin in our own life and in the lives of people God places around us. There are not many clear answers about how to best apply these principles. The way these principles are applied varies on a case by case basis. There are a lot of factors that have to be considered when we make decisions related to this issue. While these issues are not easy to figure out, there is brilliantly good news of which we must remind ourselves: we do not have to figure this out. If we ask, God will give us the wisdom we need to figure how best to apply this knowledge in our life. If we ask God for wisdom with the intent of acting on what he tells us to do, he will give us what we need in order to deal with the situation. Not all sins are equal, but all sins are forgivable for those who are placing their trust in Jesus. May God help us grow in his grace. May God help us fight sin with the knowledge that what he began in us by his grace, he will also bring to completion by his grace.

Faith Works (James 2:14-26)

Additional Reading: Luke 12:32-34; Hebrews 11:6

Alex received a large sum of money from his father as a gift. Alex's father put three million dollars in a bank account Alex could access at any time. His dad gave him the account information and a debit card to access the money whenever he wanted. Alex is an artist. He does excellent works of art—true masterpieces. Alex's work as an artist does not provide a steady income for him, so he frequently has to work two or three jobs just to pay his bills. Alex recently got evicted from his apartment. Alex says he believes he has three million dollars in the bank that he is free to spend whenever he wants. If Alex really believes he has three million dollars in the bank, then why is he homeless? Why did Alex not access the money and pay the rent? Although Alex says he believes he has three million dollars in the bank, his actions betray his words. His actions reveal what he really believes.

James was writing to Christians who seem to have the same understanding of faith that Alex does. Whereas the Apostle Paul wrote his letters to object to offering dead works to God, James wrote his letter to object to offering dead faith to God. James set out to show people the nature of the type of faith that shows we are saved. True faith is evident through our actions. There is no other way that faith can be evident than through our actions. Our actions reveal what we truly believe. We do the things we do because of what we believe at the deepest level of any given moment. This is why we sometimes make choices that are inconsistent with what we say we believe. Whatever we believe most deeply at a given moment controls what we will choose in that instance.

Faith is produced in our heart through God's word soaking deeper and deeper into our hearts. Acknowledging the true God is a place to start, but that type of faith cannot save us. Every demon in hell believes in the true God, but it does not help them one bit. The Westminster Confession of Faith gives wonderful descriptions of the nature of real faith.

> "By this faith, a Christian believeth to be true whatsoever is revealed in the Word, for the authority of God himself speaking therein; and acteth differently upon that which each particular passage thereof containeth; yielding obedience to the commands, trembling at the threatenings, and embracing the promises of God for this life, and that which is to come. But the principal acts of saving faith are accepting, receiving, and resting upon Christ alone for justification, sanctification, and eternal life, by virtue of the covenant of grace."[3]

> "Repentance unto life is an evangelical grace, the doctrine whereof is to be preached by every minister of the gospel, as well as that of faith in Christ."

> By it, a sinner, out of the sight and sense not only of the danger, but also of the filthiness and odiousness of his sins, as contrary to the holy nature, and righteous law of God; and upon the apprehension of his mercy in Christ to such as

94

are penitent, so grieves for, and hates his sins, as to turn from them all unto God, purposing and endeavoring to walk with him in all the ways of his commandments."[4]

The absence of obedience to God is evidence we do not truly have faith. We are in right standing with God through faith alone apart from any works, but the faith that makes us right with God does not exist apart from works. What this means is real faith in Christ always results in action. Real faith in Christ always produces good works in our life. Real faith produces works.

When we have truly been persuaded of the truth of the gospel, we begin to live our life for God's Kingdom. We are grasped by an invisible kingdom that transcends the here and now. We see an eternal perspective of life that moves us to use our time, energy and resources for purposes that are bigger than our own life. We use our life to accomplish things that will outlive our life. Sin produces in us a ruthless, relentless devotion to our own kingdom. This selfishness that has diseased our hearts is pathological. The faith that the gospel produces inside of us is the only thing that breaks our devotion to self. The love, acceptance and forgiveness God extends to us in Jesus gives us freedom from our selfishness, guilt and shame so we can be free to do the thing we were created to do: to glorify God and enjoy him forever.

The Faith of Abraham
(James 2:20-24)

Additional Reading: Hebrews 11:17-19; Genesis 15:1-6;
22:1-19

Michael Jordan. No other name comes close to representing basketball better than that name. There are not many people in the world who haven't heard of Michael Jordan. Michael Jordan is a household name; a name associated with greatness. There used to be an advertisement that said, "I want to be like Mike!" The advertisement was pointing out how the greatness of Michael Jordan is worth imitating.

Although the name Abraham means nothing to us, to the Jewish Christians James was writing to it was a name of sheer greatness. Almost no one in Jewish history was of greater importance than Abraham. He was a man of great significance. Abraham's significance was brought even more to the forefront with the coming of Jesus. Abraham was promised that the Messiah would come through his descendants. Jesus is the promised Messiah. Abraham believed God about the promised Messiah. God credited Abraham's faith as righteousness. Abraham's faith in the promised Messiah made him right with God.

Although Abraham did not live to see the day Jesus the Messiah came into the world, God provided Abraham an earthly picture of this coming reality by providing a son for Abraham and his wife Serah when they were past their childbearing years. God tested Abraham's faith by asking him to sacrifice his son.

God was doing this to point Abraham to Jesus and the real sacrifice that would be given to save God's people. God put Abraham to the test so that the genuine nature of Abraham's faith would be shown. Abraham staked everything on God's promise.

Abraham withheld nothing from God. Abraham was seized by an invisible reality. He perceived as real fact that which was not revealed to his senses. He was awakened to and convinced of the reality of God's promise. He was willing to put everything on the line because he was convinced that God was able to do what he had promised. Abraham's faith was living and active. His faith sparked something inside of him that moved him to action. His faith in God's promise shows us that true faith moves us to action. May God awaken us to the reality of his promise so that we live our life looking through the lens of his goodness and the hope that he has given to us. May we catch a vision of heaven that transforms the way we live today here on earth.

God Saves Bad People
(James 2:24-26)

Additional Reading: Hebrews 11:31; Joshua 2:1-22; 6:23;
Matthew 1:1-6

The wonderful thing about God saving people through faith is no one is beyond his saving reach. When the twelve Israelite spies went to check out the land God had promised to them, they came across a prostitute named Rahab. Rahab had heard about the great and mighty deeds of the God of Israel. This led her to put her trust in the God of Israel. Her trust in the God of Israel was made evident through her act of hiding the spies to protect them from danger. God blessed her faith by saving her and her family from the destruction that would happen when God's people would capture the Promise Land and destroy their enemies living there.

God not only saved Rahab and her family from destruction, Rahab was also blessed to be included in Jesus' family tree. Jesus was one of Rahab's descendants. An unsuspecting prostitute who worshipped false gods turned to the God of Israel to save her. Little did she know she would prepare the way for the God of Israel to enter into our world as a human baby. The God who would be delivered out of the womb of one of her relatives would one day deliver her in the most ultimate way possible by saving her from her sin. Rahab's faith prompted her to action. Her actions had an effect that was of eternal significance. Her faith led to events that changed the entire course of history and the fate of the human race. God abundantly blessed an ordinary, broken woman who saw her need for God to save her. She was a prostitute who acted in faith.

God is still doing the same type of things today. God will bless us above and beyond all we can ask or imagine when we abandon living for our kingdom and stake everything we have on God and his promises. God is not looking for us to simply agree with what he says and then go about our usual business. Real faith—the faith that God desires—sees the promises of God in such a way that we perceive the invisible reality of his promises as real facts we can entrust ourselves to and stake our very lives upon. The essence of faith is being seized by a divine, invisible reality in such a way that the goodness of God and the blessing we receive by seeking him move us to act in ways that display the reality of the truth of his promises.

God is able to awaken this type of faith in anyone. No one is beyond God's reach. God is able and willing to meet anyone right where they are. God is able to reach down right where we are in the middle of our mess and awaken us to a wonderful reality that we were previously blind to. Everyone who calls upon the name of the Lord will be saved—no exceptions. Is your life a mess? Are you living in a way that is completely the opposite of how you know you are supposed to live? Are you broken? Do you know that you are helpless to change yourself? God is able and willing to help those who know that they cannot help themselves. God is able to do huge, miraculous things through ordinary, messed up people who turn to him and put their trust in him. Rahab was a professional slut. She got paid to have sex with people. Yet look at what God did through her and her family. God shattered the cycle of brokenness that

99

was in Rahab's family. When God saved Rahab, she and her family became part of God's people. It was through Rahab's family that Jesus Christ was born. Never underestimate the power of God to do amazing things through people who know they need him.

Teaching is Serious Business (James 3:1)

Additional Reading: Luke 12:48; Matthew 5:17-19; 18:1-6; 12:33-37

Words. One of the things that separates the human race from the rest of creation. We like to talk. We talk a lot. Not only do we just speak words, we actually communicate meaning through our words. Our words reveal realities that cannot be touched or seen. Words shape and influence our life and the lives of the people around us. Think of some of the moments from your life. Some of our most powerful memories are of something someone said to us. We have memories where we remember exactly what someone said to us a long time ago—the exact words. Sometimes words are spoken that burn painful or joyous moments into our mind—memories we never forget. Proverbs 18:21 tells us, "Death and life are in the power of the tongue: and they that love it shall eat the fruit thereof." Our words have power. Our words can heal and bring life. Our words can wound and destroy. Our words have a tremendous impact on the people and situations around us.

James begins chapter 3 reminding the people he is leading of the weightiness of being part of the church's teaching ministry. James mentions that teachers will be judged with greater strictness. What James is NOT saying is that a teacher's salvation is dependent upon how well they fulfill that role. We are saved solely because of what Jesus did for us. We are not saved because of what we do. We are saved because of what Jesus did. While it is true that we are not saved on the basis of our works, it is also true that we will be judged according to our works. How this works out practically is that Christians will be rewarded for their acts of obedience, as imperfect as those acts may be. Our salvation is certain because it is based on what Jesus did. The reward God gives to us for our obedience is just the icing on the cake of salvation we already possess. The cake itself is what Christ has done. The cake is finished. We can't add to our cake in any way. Our acts of obedience are just the icing that has been put on top of our cake. Our obedience makes our salvation taste so much sweeter. It does not change anything about the cake itself. But the icing does help us to enjoy the cake more.

James is telling us that those who teach in the church will undergo a stricter judgment of their works than people who don't teach. We are accountable for everything that has been entrusted to us. The more entrusted to us, the more God expects from us. Those who teach God's people have a tremendous responsibility. What they say, do and teach has an immense amount of influence over a large group of people.

Not only do teachers have a lot of influence over a large group of people, they are also called to be God's voice to his people. They are called to speak on God's behalf by accurately presenting the meaning of what he says to us in Scripture. Teachers are stewards of the gospel. They are entrusted with the task of proclaiming to people the way to life. They are entrusted with delivering a message that comes from the King of kings. It is a message that brings life and freedom. It is a message that opens and shuts the only door to heaven and eternal life on those who hear it.

Being able to have the privilege to teach God's people comes with great responsibility. Some of God's worst judgment is reserved for false teachers who do not truly know Christ; people who claim to be a Christian, yet teach God's people ideas that are contrary to what he has told us in Scripture. Such people await a horrific eternity.

> **"But these speak evil of those things which they know not: but what they know naturally, as brute beasts, in those things they corrupt themselves. Woe unto them! for they have gone in the way of Cain, and ran greedily after the error of Balaam for reward, and perished in the gainsaying of Core. These are spots in your feasts of charity, when they feast with you, feeding themselves without fear: clouds they are without water, carried about of winds; trees whose fruit withereth, without fruit, twice dead, plucked up by the roots; Raging waves of the sea, foaming out their own shame; wandering stars, to whom is reserved the blackness of darkness for ever."** Jude 10-13

Claiming to be speaking for God while misrepresenting who he is and what he has said is so heinous to God because it leads people away from him in such a way they often do not even know they are being misled. Receiving false teaching into our life is dangerous because our beliefs shape the way we think and the decisions we make. When we believe things that are not true, our life will inevitably be affected in a negative way. Many people's lives have been ruined because of false teaching.

Only the gospel can set people free. People who have been entrusted with the task of proclaiming the gospel to God's people have been given a tremendous privilege and responsibility. Being entrusted with the task of teaching God's people is a blessing that should not be entered into lightly. For to whom much is given, much is expected.

The Word War (James 3:1-12)

Additional Reading: Romans 7:15-25; Matthew 12:34; Luke 6:43-45

     Some days it seems as though the only time I open my mouth is to switch feet. I have a ferocious habit of putting my foot in my mouth. My mouth often proves to be a major source of frustration and blessing. I say things I ought not say. And I say a lot of encouraging things as well. Words are my biggest gift and biggest struggle. I wrestle everyday with what comes out of my mouth. We live in a world of talk. As people, we love to talk. We do it all the time. Some of us even talk when we have nothing to say. Words are a large part of our life. Much of our life is wrapped-up in words. Our lives would be very different if there were no such thing as words. Our world of talk brings with it many good things. But, as we all know from experience, our world of talk is also a world of trouble. Some of our deepest wounds revolve around something someone said to us. Some of our deepest regrets revolve around something we said. Words have destroyed many families and friendships. Words have ruined successful businesses. Words have brought nations to war. Day in and day out, our words wreak havoc in our lives in some way or another. We face "talk trouble" every day of our life.

     Why does our world of words cause us a world of trouble? Why do we struggle so much with words? After all, our words even direct the course of our life and have great influence over us. The real reason we often cannot control what comes out of our mouth is because what comes out ties directly to our heart.

What comes out of our mouth reveals what is in our heart.

As believers, our mouth often serves to reveal the inconsistencies in our heart. Our words reveal our faith and our hypocrisy. Our words reveal what is really going on in our heart. If our mouth is continually spouting out a polluted message, it is likely the case that we have not been born again. It is likely that God has not truly changed us if the message that comes out of our mouth has not changed either. When God truly changes a person by breathing spiritual life into them, their words change. Claiming to have a new heart while having a mouth that pours out a polluted message is like saying apple trees produce onions. It simply cannot happen. The inconsistencies are far too great to reconcile.

James tells us that a perfect person can control their tongue. He also tells us no human being can control their tongue. James is asking us to do something we have no ability to do. How can he tell us to do something with which we have no ability? What hope does this give us?

While no human being can tame the tongue, the Holy Spirit is able to do this. Through prayer and the miraculous heart change that only the Holy Spirit can produce, we can begin to have more control over what we say. Though we have no inherent ability to control what we say, God is able to accomplish in and through us what we are not able to do for ourselves. Getting control over the words that come out of our mouth is an uphill battle. It is not an easy task. It is a fierce battle that is being fought in the depths of our heart. It is a battle that is impossible to win in our own strength. Yet because of what Jesus has already done for us, it is a victory we already have. In our war

106

of words, we fight *from* victory rather than *for* victory. Jesus is the Word of God. He is our ally in our war of words. Because Jesus, the Word of God, has already won the victory over sin, death and hell, our heart can be changed, which means the things we say can change. Because of Jesus, the Word of God, we can have victory over our words. Our words can be overtaken by the power of the love of the Word so that we start to reflect who he is with the way that we talk. The more we receive God's love for us, the more our heart and words will change. The love of God has the power to change how we talk in ways that will reflect who he is more and more. And that is something worth praising God about.

The Heart of Wisdom (James 3:13-18)

There was once a soldier who took great delight in his commander. One day while the soldier had a day off from battle he went out to gather blackberries to give to his commander as a token of his appreciation for the commander's leadership. The commander did not particularly like blackberries but was thrilled by the soldier's gesture. He gave the soldier three extra days off for his thoughtful gift. One of the soldiers who saw what happened thought to himself, "I know what I'll do. If the commander will reward a simple gift of blackberries, surely he will give me an even bigger reward if I get him a bigger and better gift. The commander loves whiskey. And I happen to have an unopened bottle of his favorite kind. Surely the commander will reward me greatly for giving him my best bottle of whiskey."

The commander was a very wise, discerning man. When the soldier gave his bottle of whiskey to his commander, the commander thanked him for the gift and then left to go finish up some paperwork. The soldier became very indignant about the commander's response. He called out to the commander, "You gave another soldier three extra days off for a lousy basket of blackberries, yet you did not give me anything for the whiskey I gave to you?!" Being the wise man he was, the commander saw right through the soldier's gesture. The commander replied, "The other soldier gave the blackberries to me. But you gave your best bottle of whiskey to yourself." And with that, the commander dismissed the soldier from his presence.

The commander saw through the gifts themselves to the motives behind why the gifts were being given. Even though the commander did not like blackberries, he was overjoyed to receive them because the soldier who gave them to him did it as an act of appreciation. That soldier was not looking for anything in return. The commander's joy was the chief end the soldier had in giving the blackberries. The soldier who gave the commander his best bottle of whiskey was not really giving it to the commander as much as he was giving it to himself. His motivation for giving the whiskey was selfish. This soldier gave the whiskey to the commander so he could benefit from giving the gift. There was no real cost for the soldier to give the commander his bottle of whiskey because the whiskey was just something he was using to get what he really wanted. The commander did not want to be used by this soldier. Though the two soldiers both offered gifts to the commander, the motives of these two men were vastly different. There was a lot going on beneath the surface that motivated the two soldiers to give gifts to the commander.

James is exhorting us to see the motives that are behind our sinful actions. James wants us to see the sin beneath the sin. He wants us to get down to the root of our sin—to why we do the things we do. And then he wants to show us what true wisdom looks like.

Several years ago there was a great detective television show called *Law & Order: Criminal Intent.* The show featured the quirky, eccentric detective named Robert Goren. Detective Goren always had unusual—sometimes even bizarre—ways of solving cases. He solved cases in ways that very few people are able to. How did he do it? He did it by getting inside of the mind of the person who committed the crime. He had the ability to look at the evidence from the crime and see the characteristics of the person who committed the crime. He saw into the motives of the person who committed the crime. He saw what type of person would have committed the crime. He understood human nature. He knew what made people tick. He saw into the depths of humanity, down to the roots of why people do the things they do.

James is like this master detective, probing the human heart, digging deep into our motives for doing the things we do. James starts off by telling us to do good works for the right reasons and in the right way. He tells us to not do good works in ways that will draw attention to ourselves. We are not to do good works as a means for personal gain. Good works are to be done for the purpose of pointing people to God. James tells us this because he knows the nature of our heart. He knows how driven we are by "bitter envying and strife in [our] hearts."

"Bitter envying" is an entitlement mentality. Sin has bred into us the idea that we have rights—that people and God owe us something. We believe we are entitled to have the good things we have. We become angry when people or circumstances violate the rules of our kingdom. We feel threatened by anything that gets in the way of us having what we think we deserve. We fight in any way we feel is necessary to ensure that we have what we think we are owed.

James also knows that we are naturally driven by "strife." Strife is the achievement mentality that is embedded in our hearts. God's law is written on our hearts. The principle of "Do this and live" rings throughout our entire being. We are driven by

110

something theologians call "works-righteousness." We are born with a principle written on the fabric of our soul that tells us that we must do something in order to get what we want or need. There are all kinds of ways we do this. The religious versions of this usually involve obeying a set of rules. When we think we are living up to our own rules, we see ourselves as successful. In this scenario, our sense of identity and worth comes from our ability to live up to the rules. There are also non-religious versions of strife. Some people get their sense of identity and worth from their job. Some people get it from their ability to win at sports. Some people get it from their popularity or social standing. Some people get it from having a significant other. The ways in which we seek to find worth and significance are endless. Regardless of the way we go about trying to earn our place in this world, an achievement mentality undergirds everything we are naturally inclined to do.

The mindset that drives us to try to earn our place in life through achieving is straight from the pit of hell. This mindset deceives us into believing we are entitled to what we perceive to be the good life. This mindset can only do one thing: destroy our life. What do "bitter envying" and "strife" produce in us? "Confusion and every evil work."

When our life is based on what we are able to do, we become jealous of anyone who threatens our status. Because there is always the possibility that someone might become better than us, there is always the risk that we might lose that status. We also want what other people have, which causes strife inside us and in our relationships. It also enslaves us to do whatever we have to in order to get what we are want. Whenever we seek to get from the world what we can only get from God, we end up becoming enslaved to the world. Instead of ruling over the things God has created (which is how God intends for us to live), the things God has created end up ruling over us. And the more we engage in this idolatry, the darker our understanding becomes. Misuse of the things God has created leads to more misuse—worse misuse. In other words, the more we misuse the things God has given to us, the more twisted our thinking becomes--which leads us into all kinds of sin and filthiness.

What does all of this reveal about the nature of wisdom? What does all of this even have to do with wisdom? Wisdom is not primarily abstract knowledge or a philosophy about life. Wisdom is primarily a heart issue. Wisdom is the right use of knowledge. We only appropriately use the knowledge we have to the degree that our heart is right with God. The degree to which the righteousness of Christ is manifested in our life is the degree to which we will exercise wisdom in our daily life. The more we become aware of the reality of what Christ has done for us, and the more we are resting in this reality rather than striving to earn our place in this world, the more wisdom we will gain. Being embraced by the love of God brings about repentance and faith, which releases us from our bondage to sin and self. It frees us to see life from God's perspective. Having God's interpretation of life allows us to see people and circumstances more clearly. Christ is our wisdom because he is first our righteousness.

Through Jesus' life, death and resurrection, we are forgiven and put in right standing with God. This revelation of grace and truth imparts to us the humility and compassion we need to effectively relate to other people. When we have a perspective of the universe where God is seen in his rightful place, we begin to come into alignment with how we were made to live. God is in the center of our universe where he rightfully belongs. Living with this type of wisdom does not guarantee a positive outcome from the people with whom we interact. However, living with this type of wisdom is the only way things can begin to be restored to how they were meant to be. The wisdom we need most is a Person: Jesus Christ. Through the freedom Jesus gives to us, wisdom is produced in us in such a way that redemption begins to manifest itself in our life. Restoration begins to happen in our life. May the love of Christ produce in us a wisdom that speaks wholeness to our foolish, broken world.

Why Can't We All Just Get Along? (James 4:1-5)

Additional Reading: Matthew 6:24

"Want...want...want...want...want..." When he raised his tremoring arm to point his crooked index finger towards the forbidden object of his desire, I knew I was headed for trouble. Not only was he a very big man, he was also as strong as an ox. And he had a stubborn streak that no mule could ever contest. Persuading him to focus on something else was almost always impossible. This man had mental disabilities. I was entrusted with the job of teaching this man skills that would help him live more independently. I witnessed this man destroy his own house several times simply because he could not get what he wanted. His wants exercised great control over him. His desires sometimes overrode any clear sense of reason.

Lest we think this man is an extraordinary example of broken humanity, perhaps we should honestly evaluate our world. Countless marriages end in divorce because the selfishness of each person drove them apart. Adults join gangs and willingly murder people for wearing the wrong color hat in their neighborhood. Business partners break up their partnership over disagreements about insignificant issues. Family members refuse to speak to one another because of minor disagreements over how a holiday should be celebrated. Friends become jealous of each other's success. Conflict is something that is part of everyone's life. There is not a person in this world whose life is free of conflict.

We say and do hurtful things to the people we love and care about. We do this almost every day in some form or fashion. Not a day goes by where we do not have a conflict of some kind. Conflict is a regular part of our life. Conflict is an unavoidable part of our world. Why does so much conflict exist? During the time of the Los Angeles riots in 1992, Rodney King asked a question that every one of us has asked at some point in our life: "Can't we all just get along?" Why do we fight so much? Why is there so much conflict in the world? Why is there so much conflict inside of us?

All sinful, human conflict is the result of one or more person seeking to find their pleasure and satisfaction somewhere other than in God. Our wants have a destructive, controlling power over us when our heart is bent toward something other than glorifying and enjoying God. When something or someone is blocking us from getting our object of desire we become willing to hurt or violate the rights of others. We will do this in order to get what we want. We will even do this because we cannot get what we want. We want to look better than someone, so we talk negatively about them. We will manipulate people and situations in our favor. We will present ourselves in a way that makes us seem better than we actually are. We will say mean or manipulative things to people who won't give us what we want. We will make our love and respect for someone dependent upon them giving us what we want. We will flatter people for personal gain. We will do the right thing for the wrong reasons. We will tell people exactly what they want to hear even if what we say is not the truth. Sadly, the degree to which we care about justice happening in a situation is largely dependent upon whether or not it is convenient for us to become involved—unless, of course, it is our rights we think are being violated. We often will do whatever it takes to get what we want. We try to usurp the role of God in our life. We try to live as though we are the captain of our own soul. We want to be the one who calls all of the shots. We do not want to be at the mercy of Another.

Instead of our life saying to others, "God has a wonderful plan for your life. Serve him", our life screams out, "I have a wonderful plan for your life. Serve me." We seek to get others to become servants of our kingdom. What happens when people will not serve our kingdom? What happens when everyone's goal is to get everyone else to serve their kingdom? Conflict is the inevitable result. Broken relationships are a symptom of a much deeper, more abiding problem that is going on inside of us.

The vast majority of the conflicts and broken relationships that are part of our life are due to the fact that our selfish desires for personal pleasure have taken control of us. The problem is not that we are pursuing personal pleasure. The problem occurs when we pursue personal pleasure apart from God. Every time a conflict or broken relationship is present, we can almost be certain that at least one of the people involved is being guided by selfish desires for personal pleasure.

How else can we tell if we are living our life for something other than the glory and enjoyment of God? Our prayer life reveals a lot about our spiritual condition. Are we praying? Are we spending time in prayer? Prayerlessness indicates that we are not looking to God to satisfy our heart. A stale prayer life indicates that we are looking elsewhere for

116

satisfaction rather than to God. A lack of prayer in our life shows that we are trying to satisfy our heart ourselves rather than waiting and depending on God.

Not only is it important to ask ourselves if we are praying, we also need to examine whether or not God is answering our prayers. God does sometimes wait to answer some of our prayers. Sometimes his answer is, "Yes, but not yet. Wait." However, if the vast majority of our prayers are going unanswered then we might be praying with wrong motives. God might be answering these prayers by telling us, "No." God will almost never answer prayers that are motivated by selfish desires. God is not a cosmic vending machine. He is not Santa Claus. God will not let us use him as a means to our end. He will not let us use him to get what we want--if what we really want is not him.

Prayers God answers are prayers that are aimed at building up God's Kingdom. Prayers God answers are prayers related to growing us (and others) spiritually. Our heart will never be satisfied with anything less than God. God loves us too much to give us anything that will not ultimately be of any lasting benefit to our life.

God will not allow us to live as dual citizens of both our kingdom and his kingdom. Part time faithfulness is not an option God has given to us. If you have a spouse who is 80 percent faithful to you yet is having sex with someone else 20 percent of the time, you would not consider your mate to be a faithful spouse. We would be astonished to hear our spouse claim that it is enough that they are faithful at least part of the time. Marriage is a type of relationship that demands that spouses be faithful to one another 100 percent of the time. There are some things in life where we must be 100 percent faithful in order for our devotion and faithfulness to truly matter.

God will not allow us to be Christ's Bride and whore around with lovers less wild than Jesus. When we open our heart to find our satisfaction and pleasure in something or someone other than in Jesus, we are committing spiritual adultery. Seeking to satisfy our heart somewhere other than in Christ causes us to whore out the core of who we are to things that will ultimately leave us empty. God's extravagant love demands our wholehearted devotion. If God demanded anything less than wholehearted devotion he would not be good. We were made to glorify God and enjoy him forever. Anything that falls short of these two connected aims will ultimately only leave us empty and destitute. No matter how faithful we are to the other lovers in our life, these other lovers will never be faithful to us. Only the love that God has given to us in Christ is able to satisfy our heart. God is faithful to us even when we are not faithful to him. He pursues us even when we reject and turn away from him.

When our heart is given over to lovers less wild than Jesus, we miss out on experiencing peace and wholeness in our life. Most of the misery, restlessness and discontentment we feel is due to the fact that we are living out of sync with whom God made us to be. The Holy Spirit brings these feelings welling up in our heart in order to draw us back to God. God's Spirit lives inside of us. He does not want part of our heart. He wants all of our heart. He will not settle for only having part of our heart. God is a jealous lover whose heart burns for his people. He will not rest until his burning passion for us consumes all of the affections of our heart.

God's love for us never quits. God loves us with a love that will never give up on us. He will not leave us alone until we are completely in love with Jesus and we see him face to face. What is your heart telling you? What are your relationships telling you? Do you have inner peace? What is your prayer life like? Are you praying? Is God answering your prayers? What do the conflicts in your life reveal about what is important to you? What areas of your life tend to bring about the most conflict? Consider these questions. Ask God to forgive you for the ways you are looking to lovers less wild than Jesus. Ask God to help you to be more faithful to Jesus. Praise God for loving and pursuing you even when you turn away from him. May God cleanse and renew our hearts with a passion for Jesus!

Look Up, Look Out (James 4:6)

Additional Reading: Hebrews 4:14-16; Luke 11:1-13

"Look within yourself, Luke." Obi-wan Kenobi would advise and remind Luke Skywalker to do this whenever he started to get into difficulties. There is a type of Star Wars mentality that runs rampant throughout our society. "Be true to yourself." "Look within yourself. The answer is already inside of you." "Everything you need to solve this problem is inside of you." The world is bent on telling us that the answers to our problems are inside ourselves. The world tells us that inside us is a toolbox of resources able to solve all of our problems. There is some measure of truth to this idea. We are able to do all kinds of wonderful things. We have innate abilities that allow us to solve all types of problems that exist outside ourselves.

While it is true that we are capable of solving all sorts of outside problems, most of the time the real problems we have exist inside us. The majority of our conflicts are due to what is happening inside. Looking for answers within ourselves to solve our problems is futile because the root of our problems almost always is due to something going on inside ourselves. Our heart wants what it wants. It sometimes has no reason. Our selfish desire for personal pleasure cannot be solved by any resource that is within us (other than the Holy Spirit). If we want freedom from the pathological selfishness that causes so much damage in our life, we do not need to look within ourselves. We need to look out and up. We must seek God. We must seek his grace. Relying on our own willpower to conquer our devotion to self is as effective as using a water gun to cool down a molten volcano that's ready to explode. It is like using a turkey baster to put out a raging forest fire. Our willpower cannot make much of a dent in overcoming the desires that are raging inside of our heart.

A first step in fighting against our selfish desires is to acknowledge that we do not have the resources to fight those desires. Then we need to acknowledge that only God can provide those resources. If we try to fight our selfish desires in our own strength we will not get very far. God will shut down any opportunity we have to prevail in this fight. When our pride wells up and leads us to act in our own strength, God will oppose and shut down our efforts. God will expose our self-righteousness for what it really is. We are not able to produce the type of change we so desperately need.

When our heart is broken by our sin and we know our inability to break free from our devotion to self, we cry out to God to forgive and help us. It is then that God begins to move in our heart and change us. When we cry out to God to help us, he gives us the grace we need in order for change to take place. We cannot produce the changes that need to take place in our life. Submitting ourselves to God by asking him for the grace to help us is the starting point for our change of heart.

God knows the temptations we face. He knows our weaknesses. He knows the circumstances that surround us. He knows the difficulties we encounter. He knows how prone we are to turn away from him. Keep asking God for the grace to overcome your selfish desires. Ask and keep asking until God gives you the grace to overcome your sin. Keep beating on the door of heaven until you receive an answer. Do not stop asking God for his help. Keep coming to God. Do not give God any rest until he answers. Do not stop asking. His grace is bigger than our selfish desires. His grace is bigger than all of the problems we are facing. Our problems are bigger than our ability to deal with them, but our problems are no match for God. God's grace is able to deal with anything that threatens to cause us to live for ourselves. Seek his grace and you will find it.

Fight it Out (James 4:6-10)

After directing us to begin our fight against selfish desires by acknowledging it's a fight we cannot win in our own strength, James takes a turn that seems a little surprising. We might expect James to say something along the lines of, "Let go and let God." We might expect James to tell us to wait upon the Lord until we see change happen. But James does not tell us to remain passive. The first step in winning our battle against selfish desires is to acknowledge our inability to overcome these desires and to cry out to God for help. But the battle does not stop there.

The next thing James tells us to do is to submit to God. He is using military language. He tells us to give our active allegiance to God. We are to turn toward God. That is the positive part of this two-part process.

Next, James tells us to resist the devil; to turn away from the devil. We have to turn away from the temptations that come into our life. One of the things this should make us aware of is the fact that there will be a fight. We should expect and be prepared for conflict with the devil. Do not be surprised when difficulties come. Do not be surprised when temptations start coming your way. Expect that this will happen. Keep in mind that the fight is not the problem. A lack of a fight is a problem. If you are not in God's army then the enemy has no reason to attack you. You are already on his side. The fact that there is a fight shows you have a spiritual heartbeat. Feeling as though you are in a battle is a good sign. It shows that you are alive. If your life is free of difficulties you should see that as a red flag. It likely means your soul is in danger. It is a sign that something is not right. Do not be surprised when difficulties come into your life. Expect them.

One of the main ways we submit to God is by drawing near to him. This is also how we resist the devil. How do we draw near to God? The first answer to this question is that we draw near to God through Jesus Christ. We draw near to God because God has already drawn near to us through Christ. We can draw near to God because he already loves and accepts us. He has forgiven us and counts us as righteous because of what Jesus has done on our behalf. Because Jesus lived a perfect life, died on the cross as our substitute and rose from the dead three days later, we have access to draw near to God.

The second answer to this question involves how we can take steps to draw near to God. One of the ways to draw near to God is through prayer. We can ask God to give us strength. We can ask God to purify our heart; to cleanse and change us. We can listen to God speak to us by spending time in his presence. Another way we can draw near to God is through hearing him speak to us through the Bible. Every time we read the Bible we are reading the very words of God. Another way we can draw near to God is by reading or listening to teaching and preaching that faithfully explains what the Bible teaches. Another way we can draw near to God is partaking of the Lord's Supper or Holy Communion. When we partake of Holy Communion, we draw near to Christ and Christ draws near to us through ordinary bread and wine. We can draw near to God by singing or listening to songs that tell us about him. We can draw near to God simply by turning our thoughts toward him. We

124

draw near to God by thinking about who he is and what he has done. We can draw near to God by drawing near to God's people. Talking to people who are more mature in their faith than we are often proves to be very beneficial. God's people are living members of the Body of Christ. The Holy Spirit gives all believers a mystical, real oneness because of their connection to Christ. The oneness that we have with Jesus gives us a oneness with each other. This oneness allows us to love and serve one another in such a way that it is as though Jesus himself is reaching down from heaven to love and serve us.

Drawing near to God produces in us repentance and faith. Repentance involves coming into agreement with God about our sin and then turning away from it. Repentance involves seeing our sin as God sees it. Drawing near to God moves us to stop doing the things God hates. Drawing near to God moves us to delight in who God is and what he has done, which leads us to start doing the things God loves. Drawing near to God helps us to focus and gain his perspective. We begin to think the thoughts God created us to have. It causes us to mourn how we have wasted our life and dishonored God by seeking life where it cannot be found. It moves us to draw near to the God who has drawn near to us in Jesus Christ. It moves us to seek God's mercy, forgiveness and grace. It moves us to want to glorify God and enjoy him forever.

When we come to God as a beggar claiming no rights of our own, God makes us inheritors of his kingdom. When we come to God in our thirst, he becomes to us living water that quenches it. When we come to God in our hunger, he fills us with good things. When we come to God in our poverty, he gives to us the riches of his kingdom. When we come to God in our nakedness, he clothes us with his righteousness. When we come to God in our dirtiness, he washes us and makes us clean. When we come to God in our brokenness, he makes us whole. When we come to God in our bondage, he sets us free. When we come to God with nothing but need, he provides for us everything. When we come to God in humility, he lifts us up. He enables us to live as we were intended to live: to glorify God and enjoy him forever.

Tearing Down the Walls
(James 4:11-12)

Additional Reading: Romans 2:1-4; 14:4

It is easier to speak about someone behind their back than to say to their face what we think or feel about them. Why is that? Why is it so easy for our mouths to get so carried away talking badly about other people? Why do we want to make ourselves look good by making others look bad? There is a tendency in each one of us that leans towards wanting to say things that tear down other people rather than building them up. Why is that the case?

We use our words to tear other people down when we want other people to give their allegiance to our kingdom. We want people to favor us and think of us more highly than the person we are talking about. We want to make ourselves look better than we actually are, so we exaggerate the things about ourselves that are good. Not only do we try to speak more highly of ourselves than is warranted, we also say things to make other people look worse than us. We say and do things that bump-up our own image and lower the image of the person we are talking about. We want to create as much space between ourselves and our competition so we will come out on top. We feel like we have to justify ourselves before other people, so we gladly do whatever we have to in order to secure the love and acceptance we are looking for.

We also use our words to tear down other people when people do not live up to our personal standards. When people do not live up to the rules of our kingdom we condemn what they are doing. We measure what they do (or don't do) by our own standards. If what they do does not agree with how we think they should be doing something, we think what they are doing is wrong. In our conceit we ascribe to ourselves the power and authority of God's law. When we make our personal standards the law people should live by, we make ourselves out to be the Lawgiver to whom they are answerable. Basically, we are saying, "I am God." When our personal standards become what we measure other people by we are trying to fulfill God's role.

Our preoccupation with our kingdom causes us to be more concerned about our own personal rules and standards than about God's law and God's Kingdom. Aside from the fact that our personal rules and standards are, in the grand scheme of things, ultimately irrelevant, our rules and standards being violated is petty compared to the reality of the degree to which we break God's law. We make the violators of our personal standards out to be monsters while we overlook the fact that we constantly fall so short of God's standards.

James is not saying we should not assess people (or ourselves) in light of God's law. James is saying we should not assess people (or ourselves) by our own personal standards. James is saying that people are not responsible to obey our rules. The only standard people are responsible to meet is God's standard.

When God's standards matter more to us than our own standards, we will not desire to gossip or tear down other people. When we are mindful of God's standards, we see our own need for mercy and grace for having fallen so short of how God intends for us to live. Seeing clearly our own shortcomings produces in us a humility that enables us to sympathize with people's shortcomings. When God's law is more important to us than our own rules, we no longer feel compelled to hold people to our own standards. We will know that we are desperately in need of forgiveness for the many ways we break God's law. Instead of desiring to hold people accountable to our standards, we will be able to see people more accurately and objectively. Because we know that we cannot live up to the standard God holds us accountable to, a love is produced in our hearts for people. We know that both they and we are broken, messed up people who are in need of a Savior.

We are not God. People are not ultimately accountable to us. When we are face to face with the standards of the One to whom we are accountable, the reality of the mercy and grace that he has given to us produces in us a humility that moves us to love and serve people rather than to gossip and tear them down. We will see people the way that God intends for us to see them. When this happens, our heart identifies with the heart of God. We taste and see that though we fall so short of how God intends for us to live, he nevertheless meets us right where we are and loves us anyway. Only when we are drawn out of our story and into God's story will we ever treat people and talk about them the way that God intends for us to. May God remind us of Whose story it is that we are a part.

Living in the Hand of God
(James 4:13-17)

Additional Reading: Proverbs 16:9

Life can change in a second. In the blink of an eye our world can be turned completely upside-down. I can remember the first time this revelation became reality for me. I was driving to school one night. I was driving down a five-lane road. The speed limit was 45 miles per hour. It was during the peak of 5 o'clock traffic. I was driving to school like I usually did every Tuesday night. I was driving along when out of nowhere a small child suddenly appeared in the middle lane and walked right into my lane. I hit my brakes and did everything I could do to avoid hitting the child. Hitting a child with a car going 45 miles per hour would most likely kill them. The child was very short. As I did my best to swerve away from him, I lost sight of him.

BUMP. BUMP. When I lost sight of the child and felt a large BUMP, I was certain I had killed him. For a span of 30 seconds what rushed through my mind was how my life, his life and the life of his family were forever changed. Those 30 seconds felt like an eternity. I was absolutely convinced that the child was dead. As I opened my car door I heard the sound of crying. Never before was the sound of loud crying such a sweet relief to hear. He was alive. Miraculously, he was alive. The injuries he sustained were very minimal—even for an accident of this type. Added to this miracle were the police and an ambulance being within walking distance of the accident. The police saw what had happened and

130

knew that there was nothing I could do to have avoided what had happened. The EMS workers immediately took the child to the hospital where he could be observed. The child was scraped-up and bruised, but other than those minimal injuries he was perfectly okay. It was that day that I learned how quickly life can change. In an instant, life as we know it can be over.

James writes to God's people to tell them about how quickly life can change. James is writing to help give them some perspective about how we should view our time here on earth. James writes to remind us of how short and fleeting life is. James reminds us that our life must be lived in the light of eternity.

James is saying a lot to us in these five verses. There is also a lot in these five verses that he is not saying. James is not saying, "Do not plan or prepare for the future." He is not saying, "Do not have ambitions and goals." He is not saying, "Do not budget." He is not saying, "Do not try to be good stewards of your resources." James is not saying any of those things. If that is what James is NOT saying, what IS James saying?

James is primarily talking about not assuming that "life as usual" is truly what is usual in life. Every day of my life I have woken up, opened my eyes and gotten out of bed. Because this has happened every day of my life, it would be natural for me to assume that this is what will happen tomorrow. But I have no guarantee that I will wake up tomorrow morning. I could die in my sleep tonight. It is a possibility. I have no guarantee that my eyes will always function how they are supposed to. I have no guarantee that my body will be able to move tomorrow morning the way that it always has. I assume that life will continue on like it always has. But just because my usual experience might lead me to assume that there are certain givens in life, this does not mean that my assumptions are correct. Life can change in the blink of an eye. This reality has a lot of implications for how we should live today.

James is talking about not assuming that life will go according to our plan. Our plan is not always the plan that God has for our life. We have a tendency to compartmentalize our life in such a way that there are areas of our life where we leave God out of the picture. There are areas of our life where we divorce our decisions from the bigger realities that confront us. We can live in such a way where it is as though we believe we have control over things we have no ability to control. We often have the illusion that we are the captains of our own life. James starts this section off by giving an everyday example of something someone might say. We could very easily picture someone in the business world in our day saying the same type of thing. This person's statement presumes upon a lot.

The person presumes upon time. He has no idea how long he will live or if he will be able to conduct business. He does not know what the future holds. You and I have no idea what the future holds for us. We have no way of predicting what will happen. We should plan and prepare for the future, but we should not live as though we know or can guarantee what will happen. Each breath we are given is a gift. We are not promised another moment here on earth.

The person presumes about place. In all likelihood there were people who were scheduled to go to a meeting in the World Trade Center on September 12, 2001. When the meeting was scheduled they had no idea that the building would not even be standing. They assumed that the building would still be there like it was two days prior. They were not wrong to schedule the meeting, but if they had built their life and meaning upon the World Trade Center still being there, their hope and joy would have crumbled with those buildings.

The person also presumes about the outcome of his actions. He very well could plan on staying somewhere for a year to make money, but he has no idea what the actual financial return will be. He could end up staying six months and end up leaving because it was the most unfruitful business decision he had ever made. The person is not wrong for having goals and a game plan. But if he believes he has more control over the outcome than he actually does he will end up being very disappointed.

One of the most amazing things in this example James gives us is that God does not factor into this person's plans at all. The person appears to be blind to the bigger realities of life. James is writing this to people who are Christians. James is pointing out how we tend to live our life with a practical atheism where God is absent from the way we think about life. It is not that we deny God's existence per say. Rather, it is that we compartmentalize our life in such a way that God is absent from the way we think about life. We make decisions where the reality of our inevitable death, God and the return of Christ are not influencing how we live our daily life. Our heart cannot be trusting both in the here and now, and in eternity. We cannot trust both in ourselves and our plans, and in God and his plans.

While it is true that God does want us to plan and use our resources wisely, we must face the fact that our future is in God's hand. We do not know what the future holds. We are finite creatures. Our knowledge and abilities are very limited. Our ability to influence the circumstances around us is limited. We have no control over the vast majority of things that happen to us. Circumstances, death or the return of Christ will inevitably interrupt most of our plans in one way or another.

We need to plan and prepare for the future. We need to have goals. We need to use our resources wisely. But there is a way in which we need to do this. Instead of focusing on our plans and assuming that we will be able to do what we set out to do, we should live our life mindful of God and the plans he might have for our life. We should not stop doing the things we are doing. Rather, we should do them with a different attitude and perspective. We should have the perspective that our life is ultimately in God's hand. We do not necessarily have to add the phrase "if the Lord wills" every time we talk about our plans. But we should think, plan and live our life mindful of the fact that we are utterly dependent on God.

In our day and time, many Christians are prone to think about God in ways that minimize his sovereignty and goodness. All of the circumstances, situations and people that come into our life are the direct result of God's will. They are there because God ordained them to be there. God is present with us and is actively involved in the world. But God has also set up history so that people and circumstances freely, yet necessarily, accomplish all that he has ordained to happen. In other words, there is no such thing as chance. God has a purpose for everything

134

that happens. Even when Judas Iscariot went against God's will by betraying Jesus, he nevertheless fulfilled God's will by doing it. We can choose to fulfill God's will like Jesus' disciple John or like Judas Iscariot, but either way we will fulfill God's will.

We ought to be mindful of God's intimate involvement in our life. We ought to see that God has a purpose in allowing things to happen the way that they do. We ought to see that our life is entirely in God's hand. We are utterly dependent on God in every way for every good thing that we have.

When we plan without factoring in God and the other large realities that confront our life, we are being arrogant. We are boasting of things we have no right to boast about. We are making ourselves out to be a god. This is a grievous thing for us to do. Part of the reason this is such an evil way for us to live is because it distracts us from obeying God in the here and now. Our preoccupation with ourselves keeps us from doing the good things we need to be doing. It causes us to miss the opportunities that are right in front of us. If our focus is on ourselves and we are determined to fulfill our plans without any consideration for what God might be asking of us, we will neglect to do what he is calling us to do. The people who come into our life do not get there by accident. The needs that we see around us are not there by accident. God has placed them in our path for a purpose. These are the people God is calling us to love and serve. These are the needs God is calling us to meet. There is no such thing as chance. The circumstances God has placed us in have a purpose. God brought them about so that we would become more like Christ and so that we would serve love and serve the people he brings into our life. If we live our life in a way that causes us to see nothing but the plans we have, we will neglect to do what God desires for us to do. While we work towards our goals and live out our plans we need to be mindful of the people and circumstances God has placed around us. There is a reason why they are there.

When our preoccupation with ourselves causes us to neglect to do good, as Christians we are disobeying God not out of ignorance, but willfully. James is ripping our excuses out of our hands. James is helping us to see the damage that sin causes. Sometimes we sin because of the things we do. But sometimes we sin because of the things we neglect to do. Sinning because of something we neglect to do can be just as bad, if not worse, than doing something that is inherently sinful. May God have mercy on us for all of the times we are so devoted to our own kingdom that we miss out on receiving the blessings he is trying to give us through doing good to those who are around us!

Making an Investment (James 5:1-6)

Are you rich? Do you consider yourself wealthy? Are you amongst the world's elite? If you live in America, your answer should be yes. We live in the wealthiest nation in the world. We live in the wealthiest nation in the history of the world. We are the wealthiest Christians in the history of the world. It is difficult for most people to consider themselves to be wealthy. Yet we have been blessed with an abundance of resources.

One of the interesting things about wealth is its ability to reveal our spiritual condition. How we use our wealth is a good indicator of where we are spiritually. James 5:1-6 deals with the issue of a wrong view and use of wealth. It is a passage that should make us very uncomfortable, especially in light of how much wealth we have.

Wealth, like all things God has created, is not a bad thing in and of itself. We must not mistakenly think that having wealth is inherently wrong. Scripture does not condemn having wealth. What Scripture does condemn is the love of money/wealth and the wrong ways we use our wealth.

It is unclear exactly whom James is directing these six verses towards. James wrote these words to people who are rich, but was he writing these words to Christians or to the unbelievers who were oppressing poor Christians? James might have been writing these words as a prophetic judgment against people who were taking advantage of these persecuted Jewish Christians. But even if James was not writing these words to believers he still felt the need for these believers to hear these words.

Therefore these words are beneficial for us to listen to and obey.

James is telling us that we should use our wealth in light of the final judgment. James portrays wealth as fleeting. He portrays hoarding wealth like hoarding bread or bananas: in a short period of time it is eventually going to rot, spoil and become useless. If we go to the grocery store and buy 50 bright, fresh, yellow bananas we will not be able to hoard these bananas. If these bananas do not get used they will rot and have to be thrown out. By their very nature they have a short shelf life. Wealth has a shelf life. Its shelf life is the day we meet our Maker, which will happen to us either when we die or when Christ returns.

One way we know we are hoarding our wealth is that we have so much stuff that we can't even use what we have. James speaks of garments that are moth-eaten. This is a good reminder of how we often have closets packed with clothes we never wear. We have countless possessions that are doing nothing but taking up space. Perhaps you have seen the television show *Hoarders* or perhaps you know people who hoard. They almost never give or throw anything away. They are people who used to own things. Now they are people who are owned by things. The things they own ended up owning them and taking them captive. When James says "their corrosion…will eat your flesh like fire" he is giving us a great picture of the enslaving nature of materialism. Over and over again in the Old Testament the prophets told God's people that those who worship idols end up becoming like those idols. Jesus tells us we cannot serve both God and money, or both God and possessions. Our devotion will either be to money/possessions or to God. We cannot successfully serve both.

The love of wealth produces in us the cancerous seeds of destruction. When deep inside us are the seeds of the love of wealth, we will reap what we have sown. When the desire for wealth has been sown into our heart we will reap wealth, but we will also reap the shelf life of wealth. We will end up with a harvest that rots and corrodes us from the inside out. The seeds start out in our soul and grow into our life and relationships. The seeds reproduce and fill our soul and relationships, and end up killing us from the inside out. Hell is the inevitable climax and result of building our life upon something that does not last. In eternity, people who built their life upon wealth are getting back the rotten, corroded harvest that is the outcome of what they were doing on earth. Eternity is a continuation and maximizing of exactly what we were doing when we were alive.

Hoarding is the result of misunderstanding why God has given us wealth. God increases what we take in so that we can increase what we give. God gives to us, enabling us to be generous and further his kingdom with what he has given us. Hoarding is misguided because it seeks satisfaction and security in things rather than in God. Only God can satisfy our heart. The only real security we have is the security we have in Christ. In Christ we have every spiritual blessing. In Christ we have been given the Kingdom of God.

The love of wealth displays itself in other ways too. If you have been given authority over something, are you using that authority to cheat people out of their time, money or resources? Are you doing this with your actions? Are you doing this by your inactions? Are you self-indulgent? Is your primary concern in life maintaining your own comfort and pleasure? Is your life focused on satisfying your own selfish desires or on furthering God's Kingdom? Do you sacrifice relationships and loving other people for endeavors that increase your wealth, comfort and pleasure? What does your bank account show you about your priorities? Are you aware of the futility of wealth? Are you using your wealth in light of the final judgment? What will your harvest be on judgment day? Are you preparing for the reward you will receive on judgment day? What does the way you spend your time and money tell you about your relationship with God?

These are questions we should consider and take to heart. We are saved solely because of what Christ has done on our behalf. But we will be rewarded for our obedience to God. We need to evaluate where our priorities are. Perhaps when we evaluate the way we use the resources God has given us we will discover we are not doing as well spiritually as we previously thought we were. Perhaps we will discover there are areas of our life in which we need God's freedom. Wealth is a wonderful servant, but an awful master. May God give us the wisdom and honesty of heart to see clearly what our use of wealth is saying about our spiritual condition!

Living for the Long Haul
(James 5:7-12)

Gardening is an act of faith. We plant something smaller than a piece of candy into the ground in hopes of being able to get back enough food to be able to eat several meals. The stock market works on this same principle. We put in a small amount of money in hopes of getting back a larger amount of money in return. This concept is known as the harvest principle. The harvest principle revolves around investing something that seems small with the intention of getting something bigger in return. Harvesting requires that we wait until the right time. The harvest principle works completely opposite of the concept of instant gratification. The harvest principle works on the principle of delayed gratification. Harvests only come after a good amount of waiting has occurred. Sometimes waiting can prove to be quite difficult.

James is writing to tell us to be patient and to persevere until the day that Christ returns. The return of Christ will be for us a day of deliverance. For God's people this will be the day when suffering ends and sin is completely obliterated. The return of Christ will also be a day of restoration. It will bring about the restoration of everything that sin has broken. In that day all things will be made new.

James speaks of a farmer who waits for the "early and the latter rain." The "early rain" softened the soil so that planting could take place. The "latter rain" came around ripening time. The latter rains made the harvest fruitful. The early rains already came. Christ coming into this world to live, die and

141

defeat death as a human being were the early rains. The Apostle Paul said that "in due time Christ died" (Romans 5:6). The phrase "in due time" means that Christ died at the right time. It means that God's timing was, and is, perfect. The life, death and resurrection of Christ was like a seed of redemption that was planted in the spiritual realm. The seed has to grow into the plant it was created to be. Through the preaching of the good news of Jesus, the Holy Spirit is causing the Kingdom of God to sprout up throughout the earth. The Holy Spirit is like the latter rains. He is making the harvest fruitful. The purpose of the delay of Christ's return is that the harvest is not yet ready. It takes time for God to reap the full harvest from what was planted when Christ came the first time.

What this should be showing us is that we need to be cultivating a mindset that is aimed at the long haul. What should be directing and guiding our perception of life and the decisions we make is the return of Christ. Jesus is coming back to establish the perfect Garden of Eden that will cover the entire earth. He is going to uproot all of the weeds that are presently keeping this world from being the way God intends for it to be. When Christ returns, all things will become how they are supposed to be. God's Kingdom will cover the entire earth. There will be no sickness. There will be no sadness. There will be no pain. There will be no fighting. There will be no death. God will wipe away every tear from our eyes. Heaven is wonderful, but there is something far greater that awaits us. When Christ returns, we will be given a new human body like the body Jesus had at his transfiguration.[5] The earth will be made new and we will live on a new earth in the presence of God. Full redemption is going to come. Christ's first coming guarantees that this will happen.

We need to fix our gaze on Christ's return and the full redemption that he is bringing with him. By doing this we will gain strength to deal with the problems we are facing today. If we only look at our problems, we will inevitably become discouraged. We will start to blame one another for our problems. We will bicker and argue over things that are not of eternal significance. We will become distracted.

We need to catch a vision of Jesus like the visions the prophets had who endured hardships for speaking in the name of the Lord. These prophets had been given a vision of the coming of Christ that was so powerful and beautiful that they gladly and patiently endured suffering. There was great reward for their endurance. Job is considered to be someone who went through immense hardships. Yet he is also someone who received back from God far more than he had ever lost. What Job lost was nothing compared to what he received from the Lord because of what he went through. Job is a person whose life is worth considering. Though Job did not endure his trials perfectly, one of the things we learn from his life is that trials ought to be viewed with the end that God has in mind. God brings trials into our life to build our character and to cause us to know him more intimately. Intimacy with God is often developed through times of difficulty.

James ends this section by telling us something very practical. Verse 12 tells us we demonstrate patience not by making big verbal promises, but by humble talk that follows through. What we say must be matched by our actions. We should not say one thing and then do another. Patient endurance is shown by speaking honestly and humbly, and then through following up by doing what we say we will do. Being aware of our own limitations and being mindful of the return of Christ helps us to endure and be who God is calling us to be.

Are there areas of your life where you are short-sighted?

Do you view your present circumstances through the lens of the return of Christ?

Are you looking for instant gratification more than you are looking for a reward that lasts?

How long will the things that frustrate or upset you truly matter? Will it matter five minutes from now? Five days from now? Five months from now? Five years from now? For eternity?

Pray Always (James 5:13)

One of the key things that makes Christianity different from almost every other religion is Christianity teaches God is not absent. Christianity teaches God is not far removed from our daily struggles. God is intimately aware of what is going on in our life. He is involved in our daily life. The God of Christianity has proven he cares. God loved the world so much that he sent his Son into our world as a human being to live as one of us. We worship the God who can identify with us. We worship the God who wants to share the ups and down of life with us.

One of the ways we share our life with God is through prayer. All of life is meant to be lived in conversation with God. In fact, this gets at the very essence of what it means to be a human being. Humans are made in the Image of God. The essence of what it means to be made in the image of God is that everything we do is done in relation to God. Humans are bound to God in their very existence because of the nature of how God made them and the purpose for which he made them. One of the implications of being made in God's image is that we were meant to have uninterrupted fellowship with God. As we go about our daily life we should seek to be mindful of God's presence, listening to what he wants to say to us.

Not only should we listen to God speaking to us, we should also come to God with our needs. We can pray for God to alleviate our suffering and change our circumstances. Sometimes God is waiting on us to pray before he will do this.

Sometimes God has a bigger purpose for our suffering than for it to be removed. Therefore we should also ask God to give us the strength to endure through our trials. Times of trials are a great opportunity for God to reveal the sin that is in our heart. Trials are a tool God uses to reveal what we are really trusting in. Trials reveal what we have really built our life upon.

Although most of the time the trials we go through are not the result of our own sin, trials do reveal the sin that is already in our heart. Asking God to reveal our sin to us during these times can provide us with a great opportunity to grow in our faith and become more mature.

Trials can help us to learn to trust God more fully. Because of how short-sighted we tend to be, we easily to forget God's larger purpose of our trials. God promises us that "all things work together for good to them that love God, to them who are the called according to his purpose" (Romans 8:28). What does this mean? This means that God is working all things together so that we will know Christ more deeply and become more like him. When trials come into our life we should ask God to give us the faith to trust his purpose. We should ask God to give us the faith and desire to believe and cling to his promises.

Sometimes what is worse than the actual trial we are going through is the attitude we bring into these unpleasant circumstances. Trusting God and his goodness puts us in a position where our attitude does not have to make our situation worse than it already is. Trials can be a great benefit to us if we allow them to bring us closer to God. Prayer can help us gain perspective over our circumstances.

What about when our life is going well? What should our response be when life is going well? Our response should be to pray. We should praise God for who he is and what he has done for us. We should thank God for all of the good things he has given to us. We should tell God how much we love him. We should tell God how good he is. Even in trials we should thank and praise God for his goodness. There is never a wrong time to praise God.

What James is getting at in this verse is that we always have a reason to be communicating with God. Everything we experience in life, whether good or bad, should be brought to God. God wants to be our constant companion who walks with us throughout all of our life. He wants to hear from us. He wants to be invited to walk through life with us. He not only wants to share in our good times, he wants to walk through every part of life with us. God is a loving Father who wants to spend time with his children. God wants to hear from you. God wants to speak to you. What do you want to say to him? What is he saying to you?

When Life is Too Much to Handle (James 5:14-18)

What happens when life becomes overwhelming? What happens when life becomes so difficult that we do not even know how to pray? What do we do when life beats us down? What do we do when we feel as though God is not hearing our prayers? What do we do when we doubt that God even cares? What should we do during times like these? Where should we turn? The answer James gives to these questions might surprise us.

James starts this section of Scripture with a question. "Is anyone among you afflicted?" The word James uses for "afflicted" includes physical illness, but it also has a much broader meaning. The word James uses is also used in Scripture to describe a weak mental ability (Romans 6:9), our spiritual condition before we met Christ (Romans 5:6) and someone's physical appearance (2 Corinthians 10:10). James is talking about the various kinds of weaknesses that result from going through trials. James is asking, "Is anyone among you beat up and worn out? Is anyone among you exhausted and worn down by difficult circumstances? Is anyone among you buckling under the weight of all of the pressure you are under?"

What does James tell us to do if this is what we are experiencing? We are to call the elders and have them pray over us and anoint us with oil in the name of the Lord. In this type of situation, the oil is being applied as a sign either of God's blessing or of the Holy Spirit. It is a sign that the person is being set apart so that God can work inside of the person to heal and strengthen them. It is a sign that the person is being marked to receive God's blessing.

Notice the people James says who are to do this praying and anointing. James says the elders are the ones who are supposed to do this task. Elders are not necessarily people who are elderly. Elders are mature men whom God has set apart to help lead his people. Elders are men of character and maturity who serve as overseers of the church.

The prayers of the elders that are made in faith are able to restore, heal and strengthen the person who is sick. Praying in faith means that we pray with the assurance that God is able and willing to answer our prayer. In general, praying in faith does not automatically guarantee that we will get what we have asked for. Our prayers are answered if it is God's will. However, if we pray for something like for God to strengthen or grow us spiritually, he will always give us what we have asked for because what we have asked for is his will for our life. When we have been weakened by the trials we are facing, is it God's will for us to be strengthened so that we can endure, persevere and overcome? This absolutely is God's will. God might not answer these prayers in the way we think he ought to, but he will always provide what we need so that we can endure and persevere.

During difficult times it often becomes easy for us to fall into sin. Old habits we used to rely on to cope with life come back into our mind. It is easy for us to fall back into patterns that are familiar and comfortable to us. During difficult times we tend to do what we used to do in the past. Ironically, the sin we seek to bring us comfort inevitably serves to weaken and wreck us even more than we already were before.

Sin grows best in darkness. This is why there is a tremendous amount of power in confessing our sins. We should make it a practice to confess our sins not only to God, but also to mature believers whom know us well and are trustworthy. Having a wise, mature believer pray and declare God's forgiveness over us is empowering. God's presence dwells richly in the midst of his people when they gather together. Healing and wholeness from sin is something Christ often brings to us through his people.

Two of the means God has given to strengthen us in our faith are prayer and his people. We will not make it far on our faith journey without using these two things to our advantage. Difficult times will come. Trials will come. And when they do, how are we going to get through them? What will sustain us? God will sustain us. But how is God most likely going to do this? God is going to sustain us through prayer and through his people. God is going to strengthen us through the prayers his people pray on our behalf.

There is great power in the prayers of God's people. Our prayers are powerful not because of whom we are, but because the God whom we are praying to is both powerful and good. Elijah was one of Israel's prophets. His story is recorded in the Old Testament. Elijah's life was marked by great victories of faith and magnificent failures. Elijah's life was marked by both confident joy and suicidal depression. Elijah was a regular person like us. His life was far from perfect. He made a lot of mistakes. Yet Elijah served a faithful God who heard his prayers. Elijah was an ordinary guy who served an extraordinary God. This extraordinary God listens to and helps ordinary people like us.

When trouble comes, lean on God in prayer. When trouble comes, lean on God through his people. We are weak, but God is both strong and good. God is never far removed from our struggles. When God seems absent, call on him in prayer and call on his people. He will meet you there.

Prone to Wander (James 5:19-20)

Additional Reading: Matthew 7:1-6; 18:15-35;
Galatians 6:1-5

When difficult seasons of life arise it is easy for us to walk away from our relationship with God. It is easy to lose heart when our faith is costing us something. During difficult times it can become easy for us to wander from the truth that we have been reconciled to God.

Turning away from our sin and turning toward Christ is not a one-time thing we must do. It is something we must continue to keep doing for the rest of our life. Lack of repentance and faith in our life is evidence we may have never been saved. People who wander from God are putting themselves in great spiritual danger. Scripture teaches that we can never lose our salvation—if we truly have it. Scripture also teaches that we must persevere to the end if we are to be saved. People who wander from the truth are in great danger.

Because of our many weaknesses and how prone we are to stumbling in our faith, we need a community of believers to help encourage us and keep us accountable. When someone wanders away from God and his people, we need to try to bring them back to the truth of the gospel so that they can get back on the right track. It is not just the role of the elders to keep God's people on the right track. It is the role of every Christian. We should continue to reach out to people who have walked away from God and his people. Neglecting to reach out to those who are straying from God is such an awful thing because it is the exact opposite of the heart of Christ, who saved us from the wrath of God by covering our sin with his blood. Jesus lived a perfect life, died and rose again so that we might have eternal life. We are called to demonstrate this same type of love to other people. Jesus came to seek and save the lost. His love for us should motivate us to do the same.

It is not a question of *if* we are to try to bring back someone who is wandering away from the Lord. The real question is *how* we are to bring back someone who is wandering from the Lord. One of the most important things we need to be mindful of is our motivation for wanting someone to return to the Lord. Are we motivated by love? Will it be evident to the person that we genuinely care about them? Will we come across as though we are coming to them because we love them?

Another thing we need to be mindful of before we go to someone wandering from the Lord is the condition of our own heart. We need to be aware of who we really are. We need to be aware of our own weaknesses and shortcomings. We need to be aware that we ourselves are just as capable of walking away from the Lord as they are. We need to be mindful of the fact that the only reason we have or do any good thing is because of the grace of God. We need to approach the person with humility and compassion. We need to approach them in a way where we are honest with them about our own struggles. We need to speak with them with gentleness. We need to speak truth that has been saturated with grace. We need to speak words that build them up in their faith. We need to remind them of the greatness of God's promises.

Speaking the truth in love to people who have wandered from the Lord is difficult to do. Loving

153

people who have wandered from the truth is not easy. Sometimes it is heartbreaking. But the reward for doing this will be great if the person returns to the Lord. The cost of not reaching out is too high for us to not try. Christ sought and saved us. His love for us should compel us to do the same for others.

An Inconclusive Conclusion?
(James 5:19-20)

James did not end his letter with any concluding remarks. Most of the letters in the New Testament end with some type of closing comments. They might say something like, "Bob and Steve send their greetings. I hope to visit you before winter. May God's peace be upon you!" Or the letter may end with something like, "I am sending my fellow worker John to you. Welcome him as though he were me. May God give you the strength to persevere!" But James just ends his letter with teaching. Why did James end his letter so suddenly? Why did James not include any closing thoughts?

We can only guess why James ended his letter the way he did. But it is not incidental that he ended his letter in this manner. If we look at the heart of what James has written about, the way he ends this letter makes perfect sense.

James probably ends his letter so suddenly because he wants us to know that there is work to be done. We are the agents through which God builds his Kingdom. The gospel has to be preached. The lost have to be reached. People have to hear the gospel and see what life in God's kingdom looks like. James writes his entire letter with a sense of urgency. His letter continually puts before us the reality of eternity. James' letter serves to remind us that we must live in a way that reflects the truth that time is short and eternity is long. His letter shows us what it looks like to not waste our life on trivial things. His letter shows us how we can live so that our life will have an eternal impact. His letter shows us that we can have an extraordinary impact by doing ordinary things.

The life of a Christian is a life that is devoted to God's kingdom. The work God has given us to do will not be over until either the day we die or the day Christ returns. God has a purpose for us being here on this earth during the time that we are here. James ends his letter so suddenly almost to say, "You have a job to do. There is a reason God has left you here on this earth. You have been given victory through what Christ did for you through his life, death and resurrection. Live your life in light of that victory. Live in this world as a citizen of the world that is to come. Live a life that demands an explanation. Eternity is hanging in the balance. Go forth and proclaim the victory that Christ has won." May God keep our hearts focused on him and his Kingdom! May we live our life in light of the victory!

Endnotes

[1] "The Great Divorce" is a great book written by C.S. Lewis. Lewis used the term "the Great Divorce" to describe the break in the relationship that originally existed between God and humanity.

[2] "When I Survey the Wondrous Cross." Words written by Isaac Watts. *Hymns and Spiritual Songs*, 1707.

[3] Westminster Confession of Faith. Chapter 14.2, Of Saving Faith.

[4] Westminster Confession of Faith. Chapter 15.1-2, Of Repentance unto Life.

[5] See Mark 9:2-13.

14664902R00084

Made in the USA
Charleston, SC
24 September 2012